KU-155-094

LISBON

ENCOUNTER

KERRY WALKER

Lisbon Encounter

Published by Lonely Planet Publications Pty Ltd
ABN 36 005 607 983

Australia	Head Office, Locked Bag 1,
	Footscray, Victoria 3011
	☎ 03 8379 8000 fax 03 8379 8111
	talk2us@lonelyplanet.com.au
USA	150 Linden St, Oakland, CA 94607
	☎ 510 250 6400
	toll free 800 275 8555
	fax 510 893 8572
	info@lonelyplanet.com
UK	2nd fl, 186 City Rd,
	London EC1V 2NT
	☎ 020 7106 2100 fax 020 7106 2101
	go@lonelyplanet.co.uk

This title was commissioned in Lonely Planet's London office and produced by: **Commissioning Editors** Korina Miller, Clifton Wilkinson **Coordinating Editor** Martine Power **Coordinating Cartographer** Peter Shields **Coordinating Layout Designer** Wibowo Rusli **Managing Editor** Brigitte Ellemor **Managing Cartographer** Mark Griffiths **Managing Layout Designers** Laura Jane, Celia Wood **Assisting Editor** Diana Saad **Assisting Cartographer** Andy Rojas **Cover Designer** Jane Hart **Project Manager** Rachel Imeson **Language Content Coordinator** Quentin Frayne **Thanks to** David Connolly, Jennifer Garrett, Evan Jones

Cover photograph Art lounge, Avenida 24 de Julho, Guido Cozzi/Corbis. **Internal photographs** p43, p74, p83, p105, p115 Kerry Walker; p16 Andy Christiani; p23 Imagestate Media Partners Limited - Impact Photos/ Alamy. All other photographs by Lonely Planet Images, and by Paul Bernhardt except p13, p18, p22, p32, p69, p145 Greg Elms.

All images are copyright of the photographers unless otherwise indicated. Many of the images in this guide are available for licensing from **Lonely Planet Images:** www.lonelyplanetimages.com.

ISBN 978 1 74104 853 7

Printed by Hang Tai Printing Company, China.

Acknowledgement Metropolitano de Lisboa Network Diagram © September 2008 Metropolitano de Lisboa, E.P.

HOW TO USE THIS BOOK
Colour-Coding & Maps
Colour-coding is used for symbols on maps and in the text that they relate to (eg all eating venues on the maps and in the text are given a green knife and fork symbol). Each neighbourhood also gets its own colour, and this is used down the edge of the page and throughout that neighbourhood section.

Shaded yellow areas on the maps denote 'areas of interest' – for their historical significance, their attractive architecture or their great bars and restaurants. We encourage you to head to these areas and just start exploring!

Prices
Multiple prices listed with reviews (eg €10/5 or €10/5/20) indicate adult/child, adult/concession or adult/child/family.

Send us your feedback We love to hear from readers – your comments help make our books better. We read every word you send us, and we always guarantee that your feedback goes straight to the appropriate authors. The most useful submissions are rewarded with a free book. To send us your updates and find out about Lonely Planet events, newsletters and travel news visit our award-winning website: **lonelyplanet.com/contact**.

Note: We may edit, reproduce and incorporate your comments in Lonely Planet products such as guidebooks, websites and digital products, so let us know if you don't want your comments reproduced or your name acknowledged. For a copy of our privacy policy visit **lonelyplanet.com/privacy**.

KERRY WALKER

Kerry's love affair with Portugal began as an intrepid 11-year-old that wanted to climb the cliffs
of the Algarve *alone*. She returned years later and
fell for Lisbon – its Atlantic light and crisp *pastéis*
(tarts), the disorientating lanes of Alfama and
locals dragging her – yeah right! – on Bairro Alto
bar crawls. She studied Portuguese translation as
part of her MA at the University of Westminster.
Born in Essex and based in Germany's Black Forest, she certainly lives up to her name, being an
avid walker. Her itchy feet have taken her to 40ish
countries, inspiring numerous articles, online
guides and around 15 travel books, including Lonely Planet's *Portugal*.

KERRY'S THANKS

Heartfelt thanks to my fiancé, soul mate and travel companion Andy
Christiani. I'm *muito obrigada* to Rafael Vieira for feeding me invaluable
tips, and to CouchSurfing ambassador Nuno Ramos. Sincere thanks
also to Carmo Botelho at Turismo de Lisboa, and to Jorge Moita, Joana
Amendoeira, Olivier, Alberto Bruno and Carlos Martins for providing
insight into life as a Lisboeta. Finally, a big thank you to Korina Miller
for entrusting me with this gig, and thanks to the entire Lonely Planet
production team.

THE PHOTOGRAPHER

Paul Bernhardt's camera has lured him to countries as diverse as Mexico,
Brazil, Lebanon, Iran and Mozambique. He cut his teeth as a press pho-
tographer in England, covering hard news, sport and features, before
leaving the UK to settle in Portugal, where he has lived for over a decade
and where he started to focus on more travel-related topics. His work has
appeared in various magazines, guidebooks and newspapers around the
world. Lisbon, his adopted city, is a frequent subject of his photo-
reportage and he never tires of rediscovering its people, its culture and
its history.

A touch of Paris in central Lisbon – Elevador de Santa Justa (p54)

CONTENTS

Why is our travel information the best in the world? It's simple: our authors are passionate, dedicated travellers. They don't take freebies in exchange for positive coverage so you can be sure the advice you're given is impartial. They travel widely to all the popular spots, and off the beaten track. They don't research using just the internet or phone. They discover new places not included in any other guidebook. They personally visit thousands of hotels, restaurants, palaces, trails, galleries, temples and more. They speak with dozens of locals every day to make sure you get the kind of insider knowledge only a local could tell you. They take pride in getting all the details right, and in telling it how it is. Think you can do it? Find out how at **lonelyplanet.com**.

THIS IS LISBON

Lisbon is light fantastic; an Atlantic light that illuminates the yellow blaze of vintage trams and glitters on the river, bounces off Manueline turrets spiralling into cobalt skies and burnishes the castle gold at dusk. Finally the world is turning *its* spotlight on Portugal's dazzling capital.

'Lisa', as locals nickname her, is a beauty but not a conventional one. She's compared to Havana with her graffiti-slashed pastel houses, all-night street parties, kamikaze drivers and hash-peddlers; San Francisco with her blue waters, rickety trams and suspension bridge; London with her shabby-chic boutiques and revamped docklands; North Africa with the medinalike Alfama. Truth is, it's hard to bottle Lisbon's spirit. Her essence is unique.

Daydreamers sipping sundowners at giddy *miradouros* (viewpoints) in Graça, sparky creatives reinterpreting vintage in Bairro Alto, nostalgics feeling the mournful wail of fado in Alfama – Lisboetas are as multifaceted as the city they inhabit. And it's easy to see why they love it. Lisbon has got looks but it's her personality that'll seduce you, with genuine friendliness, infectious energy and surprise elements that keep you wanting more.

Shaped by a rollercoaster history that embraces theatre-going Romans, salt-encrusted explorers and Salazar dictatorship shackles, and influenced by former colonies in Brazil, Asia and Africa, Lisbon is a cultural one-off. Where else can you find grizzled men and vibrantly dressed Angolans sipping *ginjinha* (cherry brandy), one-pan family bistros alongside Zen-style sushi bars or retro tinned-fish shops next to cutting-edge design stores?

Neither time- nor trend-obsessed, locals like to keep it real. Sure, there are enchanting palaces, Unesco-listed monasteries and galleries galore, but to truly experience Lisbon, try to luxuriate in the everyday. Saunter Alfama's alleys where neighbours gossip over citrus-scented laundry. Be swept up in Santa Catarina street parties. Twist your tongue over Portuguese vowels and creamy *pastéis* (tarts). See the light, grab your camera, live the action.

Top Ice-cream seller awaiting the crowds at the Praça do Comércio (p54) **Bottom** Sampling Lisbon's culinary delights at A Baiuca (p73) in Alfama

>HIGHLIGHTS

Enjoying a much-loved Lisbon tradition – a few drinks on the well-worn cobbles of Bairro Alto

>1 ALFAMA

GETTING LOST IN THE SIMPLY MOORISH ALFAMA

Though most of Lisbon fell like a pack of cards in the 1755 earth-quake, the medinalike Alfama drew the joker – emerging unscathed and grinning thanks to its rock-solid foundations. These cobbles have been worn smooth by theatre-going Romans, bath-loving Moors who called it *al-hamma* (Arabic for 'springs'), and the stampeding Crusaders in 1147. Now it's your turn to give them a polish.

And there's no place like Alfama for ditching the map to wander aimlessly through streets full of beauty and banter. Its higgledy-piggledy heart is laced with narrow *travessas* (lanes) carved into the hillside and twisting *becos* (blind alleys), which lead you on a spectacular wild goose chase past skinny houses in sherbet-lemon and candyfloss-pink hues. Poking around its lucky dip of lanes might reveal freshly washed underpants out to dry, neighbours dishing the latest *mexericos* (gossip), sun-baked chapels or palm-shaded *praças* (plazas) where fountains gurgle. Everywhere, walkers are rewarded with snapshot vistas down to the Rio Tejo and tantalising glimpses up towards the fortified Castelo de São Jorge (p65; above).

Crowd-pullers feature the tiled cloisters of Igreja de São Vicente da Fora (p65) and the pyramid-chequered Casa dos Bicos (p65), Afonso de Albuquerque's wacky 16th-century abode. You'll also want your

camera handy to snap the honey bricks of Romanesque Sé cathedral (p69) and the top-of-Lisbon views from precipitous Miradouro da Senhora do Monte (p65). After ticking off the biggies, pause to absorb the atmosphere over an alfresco sardine lunch at Porta d'Alfama (p72) before the streets fall into their siesta slumber.

You can lose your heart to Alfama by day, but to feel its soul return by night to hear fado in its rightful birthplace. Locals say fado captures the spirit of Lisbon with its melancholic songs about bullfighting, jealous lovers and husbands lost at sea – all mixed with a drop of *saudade* (nostalgic longing). Professional *fadistas* wow audiences in the vaults of Clube de Fado (p73), but for gutsy *fado vadio* (amateur fado) check out A Baîuca (p73). Huddled in a radiantly old-world fado bar, it seems Alfama is but a village and you're part of the extended *família*.

ALFAMA SOUNDTRACK
> Fresh sardines sizzling on open grills
> Plump matrons spontaneously erupting into wailful fado
> Footsteps echoing in sun-dappled alleys
> The shake, rattle and roll of tram 28
> Four maids a-cackling, three cats a-meowing, two church bells ringing and a pigeon in an orange tree

HIGHLIGHTS

>2 BAIRRO ALTO

BAR-CRAWLING PAST YOUR BEDTIME IN BAIRRO ALTO

When young, male Lisboetas tell their grandparents they're off to Bairro Alto many tut, shake their heads and ask why they can't get a *nice* girlfriend. For years, this working-class district was the place to throw off your Salazar straitjacket and indulge in a little after-dark sleaze. And while call girls no longer prowl these dark alleyways, the libertine is still alive 'n' kickin': graffitied slums have morphed into shabby-chic boutiques and alternative arts venues, appetising little bistros and hobbit-sized bars with an inviting glow.

Bairro Alto is Lisbon's chameleon: lacklustre and as dead as a disused theatre by day, come twilight the nocturnal hedonist rears its sleepy head. Lanterns are flicked on, shutters raised, garlic wafts from basement kitchens, fado drifts from folksy restaurants and *taxistas* (taxi drivers) hurtle through the grid of narrow lanes, forcing pedestrians to jump aside like grasshoppers in a tractor's path. The scene is set for sizzling parties and yet another *noite en claro* (sleepless night).

Our ultimate Bairro Alto bar crawl kicks off with Santa Catarina sundowners at hipster hangout Noobai Café (p49) for knockout views over Lisbon's twinkling skyline. By midnight, the street party is in full swing around Rua do Norte, Rua da Atalaia, and Rua do Diário de Noticias, where wall-to-wall bars out-decibel each other spinning merengue and rock, '80s grooves and minimalist techno. Portas Largas (p49) fizzes with *caipirinha*-sipping revellers psyching themselves up for sweaty clubbing at Frágil (p50) over the road. Retro kids slide over to Bicaense (p48) in Santa Catarina, or Ginjinha das Gáveas (p48), where cheap drinks, sticky floors and good vibes scream student house party.

THE BAIRRO EXPERIENCE
> Cursing the cobbles at 10pm and rolling down them as happy as Larry at 6am
> Sloshing your plastic cup of Sagres or sangria over your newfound amigos
> Beating off the louche guys pedalling fake hash and Rolexes on every corner
> Three magic words at 4am: who's for Lux?
> Hangover like a porcupine waltzing in your head? *Bica* (espresso) and *pastéis de nata* (custard tarts) work wonders

Cranked-up, flirty and attitude-free, Bairro Alto in the wee hours is Rio carnival meets Glastonbury: the *festa* (party) is on the street and everyone is welcome. Take the lead of easygoing Lisboetas and head outside to meet, drink and be merry, before shuffling over to Music Box (p50) for early-morning gigs, or Lux (p75; above) for high-octane clubbing down by the river. No wonder Bairro Alto looks so hung-over during the day; even party animals need to get their beauty sleep…

HIGHLIGHTS

>3 TRAM 28

SCOOTING THROUGH LISBON ON TRAM 28

Tram 28 is Lisbon's perfect fairground attraction. With its polished wood panelling, bee-yellow paintjob and gleaming chrome fittings, it's the full-scale model of a fastidious Hornby collector. Remember the scenic railway, bumpy dodgem and triple-looping rollercoaster at the local amusement park? Combine all three and you have tram 28 (minus the loops). The ride from Campo Ourique to Martim Moniz is 45 minutes of astonishing views, jolting madness and absurdly steep climbs.

Picture the scene: the tram bowls merrily along, brakes hissing and passengers lurching as the rococo dome of Basílica da Estrela (p112) and the palms of Jardim da Estrela (p112) slide into view. It scoots down the leafy avenues of Estrela, affording snatched glimpses of the blue Tejo, pausing briefly at Praça Luís de Camões. Trundling through Baixa's streets, lined with grand Pombaline edifices, it stops to let on the happy sunscreen-shiny crowds, packing them in like sardines.

How pretty, you muse, as tram 28 groans mechanically and begins its rattling climb to Alfama, where pastel-coloured houses speckle the hillside and passengers lean perilously out of the window for that in-motion shot of Sé cathedral (p69). There's a flutter of excitement as it scales the hill, hurtling around hairpin bends, tram surfers clinging to the doors like Stickle Bricks. A *senhora* (woman) makes a dash across the tracks – it's a near miss and as the tram screeches to a halt, passengers emit a pfff of relief and the driver flashes an in-control Clark Kent smile.

It's beautiful slow motion now, as the tram crests the hill at Largo das Portas do Sol (p65). Above rises the fortified Castelo de São Jorge

TRAM-TASTIC MOMENTS
> Inching open the window for closer views and just missing that wrought-iron lantern – ouch!
> That pathetic tinkle of a bell when what's really needed is a here-comes-the-tram horn
> Adrenaline-crazed tram surfers: they're fast, fearless and there's one on a door near you...
> Using elbows, *bom dias* and powers of persuasion to bag a space by the window
> Shutterbug favourites: Basílica da Estrela, Sé, Castelo de São Jorge and Alfama

(p65), while below Alfama unfurls like a magic carpet, embroidered with a mosaic of red rooftops and candy-hued houses. Tram 28 gathers momentum again as it negotiates the steep, narrow streets up to Largo da Graça, where most folk hop off to explore the serene cloisters of Igreja de São Vicente da Fora (p65).

Now where else can you experience that much exhilaration *and* tick off all the major sights? No wonder big kids want to have another go.

>4 A GINJINHA

SIPPING SUNDOWN GINJINHAS ON LARGO DE SÃO DOMINGOS

Come dusk when the light softens, locals spill onto the sticky cobbles in front of closetlike A Ginjinha (p60; above), nursing shots of *ginjinha* (cherry brandy). Cherry brandy we hear you scoff? Ah yes, but forget those memories of sickly festive tipples, this is the real deal. In the 1840s a friar named Espinheira experimented by fermenting sour *ginja* cherries in brandy; it went down a treat. The quaffing cleric still keeps beady watch over Lisbon's first *ginjinha* bar, where locals from old men in flatcaps to canoodling couples grapple for €1 to buy that minute of unadulterated cherry-licking, pip-spitting pleasure.

Take this as your cue to do the same and order one *sem* (without) or, for a kick, *com* (with) the cherry. Let's be honest, *ginjinha* is the Marmite of the liqueur world – you're either grimacing or licking the glass. But it's less about the grog and more about the event: from the guy lining 'em up at the bar to carrying your plastic cup without slopping and, of course, the spectacle on Largo de São Domingos. African mamas in bold scarlets and yellows breeze past like exotic butterflies, Brazilian beats mix with the hum of chatter, the castle glows gold on the hillside. It's captivating; particularly after a *ginjinha* or three when you're feeling as poetic as Pessoa…

>5 OCEANÁRIO

SCUBA DIVING WITHOUT GETTING WET AT OCEANÁRIO

No amount of hyperbole about Europe's second-largest aquarium where 8000 species splash in seven million litres of seawater (blub, blub, blub) could ever convey the eye-popping scale of Lisbon's Oceanário (p91). In vast wraparound tanks, honeycombed rays glide, schools of neon fish dance like aquatic strobe lights – a flash of electric blue here, a hot pink spark there – and overexcited nippers yell *tubarão!* (shark!), as Jaws Junior attempts to chomp their pinkies through the plexiglass.

So what's the fuss about fins? Hogging the limelight are superstar sea otters Eusebio and Amália, making crowds go gooey when they show off their flippers turning somersaults. Other stunners are Magellan penguins on ice, camera-shy filigree seadragons, big 'n' dopey ocean sunfish, all-tentacle giant pacific octopuses and moon jellyfish – the flying saucers of the underwater world. Accompanying the critters are encyclopaedic facts like 'sea otters have the thickest fur coats in the world'. The upshot is an aquarium with impeccable ecocredentials, realistic habitats, no circus hoopla and – ahhh – seriously happy fish.

>6 MOSTEIRO DOS JERÓNIMOS

FEASTING ON MANUELINE ARCHITECTURE AT MOSTEIRO DOS JERÓNIMOS

Expect architectural fireworks at Lisbon's finest Manueline confection, Mosteiro dos Jerónimos (p80). The lacy stonework of this early-16th-century monastery is as fine as piped icing on a wedding cake, dripping with organic detail, from scalloped arches to twisting auger-shell turrets and columns intertwined with leaves, vines and knots. Its almost edible sugariness even had Unesco licking their fingertips in 1983.

The oohs and the aahs come as you enter the arcaded cloisters, spellbinding in intricacy and rich in symbolism; look for fantastical winged monkeys and wild boars on the upper balustrade. No matter how sweltering the day, the arcades offer cool respite and a play of dark and light that would inspire Caravaggio to whip out his oils. The church is a riot of trunklike columns that grow into a vaulted web of gold-tinged stone. Just wow.

Manuel I had the marvel built in 1501 to trumpet the navigational triumph of Vasco da Gama, he who set sail for Africa in 1497 and returned – metaphorically speaking – with India. So what to do with all that pepper and cinnamon dosh but parade on an elephant, send the Pope a rhino and create the fairest monastery of them all? Jerónimos flashes back to the Age of Discovery; to voyages in a world still unexplored; to the romance of spice-scented lands. It's love at first sight.

>7 PASTELARIAS

HAVING YOUR CAKE AND EATING IT TOO AT LISBON'S OLD-WORLD PASTELARIAS

Pastelarias (pastry shops) are to Lisbon what pubs are to London: never more than a few paces away and full of sinful treats that leave you slightly poorer, a kilo heavier and *much* merrier. Initiation to this age-old, cake-scoffing tradition begins with *pastéis de nata*, the finest baked to a top-secret recipe in Antiga Confeitaria de Belém (p82; above). Since 1837, they have refined the art with precise geometry: silky, light cream (not overly sweet), a beautiful golden crust, caramelised pastry layers that flake just so; all hallmarks of perfect *pastéis*. Yet it is the experience that'll hook you – whiffs of freshly roasted *bica* curling around your nostrils, art-nouveau mirrors reflecting gilded opulence and your expanding waistline, swivelling to the stranger next to you at the polished counter to share sticky laughs in broken Portuguese, and the forlorn, glistening glob of cream on the plate as you leave. Mmmm…no wonder Lisboetas are such *pastelaria* junkies. Send that sugar and caffeine galloping to your bloodstream at old-school favourites such as Confeitaria Nacional (p58), Versailles (p106) and Pastelaria São Roque (p47).

HIGHLIGHTS

>8 MIRADOUROS

CLIMBING STAIRWAYS TO HEAVENLY MIRADOUROS

You'll huff and you'll puff and you'll curse this hilly town, but take heart in the fact that Lisbon's winding *calçadas* (stairways) and steep cobbled streets lead to magical *miradouros* (viewpoints), affording hawk's-eye views of the city. Sure, it's fun to hop aboard nostalgic funiculars, but when God gave Lisboetas *pastéis de nata*, surely he intended for them to work off the sweeties with a brisk uphill stride.

Lisbon's breathtaking *miradouros* make every steaming step worthwhile. Young, alternative types gather at Miradouro de Santa Catarina (p40) to bash out rhythms, sip Sagres and get happy on cracking views of Ponte 25 de Abril interlaced by the Tejo's ribbon of blue. For something Moorish, head up to Largo das Portas do Sol (p65) to strike a pose with the higgledy-piggledy Alfama and the Panteão Nacional's curvy dome in the backdrop. Other heart-stealers include Miradouro de São Pedro de Alcântara (p40) with its gurgling fountains and sweeping vistas across Lisbon to Sé, and highest of the high Miradouro da Senhora do Monte (p65) for the finest perspectives of Castelo de São Jorge's battlements.

>9 MUSEU DO ORIENTE

HUNTING FOR COLONIAL TREASURES AT MUSEU DO ORIENTE

If you've only time for one museum in Lisbon, make it this new dock-side gem: a 1940s *bacalhau* (dried cod) warehouse revamped into a treasure-trove of Asian riches. Opened in 2008, Museu do Oriente turns the spotlight on Portugal's ties with Asia: from the first colonial footprints of bedraggled explorers in Macau to its ongoing fascination with Asian gods.

The wondrous collection will catapult you back to the Age of Discovery in China gazing upon exquisite 16th-century lacquer-work, Ming porcelain and hand-painted silk fans. Or East Timor inspecting such curiosities as the future-predicting divining conch and delicately carved umbilical-cord knives to separate newborns from their ancestors. Head upstairs for supernatural encounters. Cult classics include Burmese Nat sculptures of 37 spirits that suffered violent deaths, dazzling Vietnamese medium costumes, peacock-feathered effigies of Yellamma (Goddess of the Fallen), and a spine-chilling, faceless Nepalese exorcism doll. For the full lowdown, see p113.

>10 PALÁCIO NACIONAL DE SINTRA

STRIKING A POSE IN FRONT OF PALÁCIO NACIONAL DE SINTRA

Unesco-listed Palácio Nacional de Sintra is more than an icon, it's the subject of heated debate: ice-cream cones, wasp nests, Madonna's pointy bra…its enormous conical chimneys set imaginations into overdrive and cameras snapping. The palace interior – a whimsical mix of Moorish and Manueline architecture – is pure fantasy, with arabesque courtyards, barley-twist columns and 16th-century geometric *azulejos* (tiles) that figure among Portugal's oldest.

Standouts include the octagonal Sala dos Cisnes (Swan Room), adorned with frescoes of 27 gold-collared swans. Suspicious? You will be upon entering the Sala das Pegas (Magpie Room), its ceiling emblazoned with magpies. Lore has it that the queen caught João I kissing one of her ladies-in-waiting. The cheeky king claimed the kisses were innocent and all '*por bem*' (for the good), then commissioned one magpie for every lady-in-waiting.

Other highlights include the wooden Sala dos Brasões, bearing the shields of 72 leading 16th-century families, the shipshape Galleon Room and the Palatine chapel featuring an Islamic mosaic floor. Finally, you reach the kitchen of twin-chimney fame, where you can almost hear the crackle of a hog roasting on a spit for the king (he didn't only have an appetite for infidelity!). Now gaze up and let the flutes work their magic… Also see p124.

>LISBON DIARY

Lisbon lives up to her mistress of revels reputation, believing *fazer a festa* (partying) is both a birthright and a rite of passage. Rio-style carnivals and catwalk shows bring smiles to lips and swivels to hips. Saintly celebrations, high-octane concerts, progressive arts fairs and indie flicks give Lisboetas reason to celebrate all year long. For up-to-date event listings, see *Time Out Lisboa* (http://timeout.sapo.pt, in Portuguese), or pick up the tourist board's free magazine *Follow Me Lisboa*.

Embracing all things ocean-themed at Lisbon's Festas dos Santos Populares (Festival of the Popular Saints; p25)

FEBRUARY

Lisbon Carnival

www.visitlisboa.com

Shake your tail feather as the samba and spirit of Rio infuse Lisbon carnival, a pre-Lenten celebration of feasting, flamboyant parades and all-night partying.

MARCH

Moda Lisboa

www.modalisboa.pt

Fashionistas make a beeline for Casino Estoril's four-day catwalk fest, where Portuguese designers from Ana Salazar to Lidja Kolovrat take their latest collections to the runway.

APRIL

Estoril Open

www.estorilopen.net

Tennis masters do battle at WTA Estoril Open, held at Estádio Nacional in Cruz Quebrada. Tickets are like gold dust, so book ahead.

Dias da Música

www.ccb.pt

Get your classical fix when world-renowned orchestras and soloists take to the stage for this three-day festival at Centro Cultural de Belém (p86).

IndieLisboa

www.indielisboa.com

Catch indie flicks on Lisbon's big screens at this 10-day filmathon, fizzing with new talent in shorts, documentaries and features. Indie Junior entertains kids.

MAY

Alkantara Festival

www.alkantarafestival.pt

The innovative, two-week Alkantara Festival lures theatre buffs with boundary-crossing performances. Hosts include Centro Cultural de Belém (p86).

Lisboa Downtown

http://lisboadowntown.sapo.pt

Freewheeling junkies tear down cobbled steps, negotiate hairpin bends and perform spectacular jumps at Alfama's boneshaking downhill race. First down gets the crown...

Rock in Rio

http://rockinrio-lisboa.sapo.pt

Lisbon's biennial Rock in Rio festival draws revellers to Parque da Bela Vista with star-studded concerts, pyrotechnics and the Cidade do Rock spinning nonstop electronica.

JUNE

Festa do Fado

www.egeac.pt

An illuminated Castelo de São Jorge (p65) stages weekends of classic and new-generation fado. Catch free fado on trams every Thursday and Sunday in June.

Lisbon Pride

www.portugalpride.org

Feel the pride as whistling, rainbow-flag-waving gays and lesbians parade from Marquês de Pombal to Praça do Municipio. Expect sizzlingly pink after-parties.

JULY

BaixAnima

Brazilian beats, jugglers and kerbside theatre – Baixa's free summertime bash entertains the ice-cream licking crowds on weekends from July to September.

Streetside festivities at the BaixAnima Festival

ALL SAINTS BRIGHT AND BEAUTIFUL

Blessed be those who worship Lisbon's centuries-old tradition of *vinho*-swigging, sardine-feasting and all-round merry-making at June's Festas dos Santos Populares (Festivals of the Popular Saints), three weeks of midsummer madness. Lisboetas embrace their saint-athon with particular gusto around Alfama, decking courtyards with multicoloured garlands. The main saintly celebrations:

Festa de Santo António St Anthony is revered from 12 to 13 June with *arraiais* (street parties), feasting, drinking and *bailes* (balls). The Casanova of saints has a reputation as a matchmaker: Lisboetas declare undying love by giving *manjericos* (basil plants) with soppy poems and around 300 hard-up couples get hitched for free!

Festa de São Pedro St Peter's festival is from 28 to 29 June and he be the patron saint of fishermen. As Lisbon has rather a lot of fish, expect fabulous feasts and raucous river processions in his barnacled honour.

Delta Tejo

www.deltatejo.com

This eco-aware, three-day festival in Alto da Ajuda rocks to mellow Brazilian grooves and Jamaican reggae under a starry sky.

Festival do Estoril

www.estorilfestival.net

The seaside playground of Estoril ditches buckets and spades in favour of strings and sopranos. Expect five weeks of outdoor gigs, opera, concerts and exhibitions.

Super Bock Super Rock
www.superbock.pt
Rocking Parque das Nações in mid-July, this headbanging, beer-guzzling shindig features a cracking line-up – previously welcoming the likes of ZZ Top, Beck and Iron Maiden.

AUGUST

Festival dos Oceanos
http://festivaldosoceanos.com
This swashbuckling fortnight revels in Lisbon's seafaring heritage with regattas, world music, riverside fireworks, kite-flying and Parque das Nações' ocean-themed parade of giant crustaceans.

Jazz em Agosto
www.musica.gulbenkian.pt
Fundação Calouste Gulbenkian (p108) shows some soul at this nine-day jazz fest of talent, both new and established, in early August.

SEPTEMBER

Festival de Cinema Gay e Lésbico
www.lisbonfilmfest.org
This is it darlings! In late September Lisbon's campest 10-day flick fest screens 100 home-grown and international gay and lesbian films. Bring your rose-tinted specs...

NOVEMBER

Arte Lisboa
www.artelisboa.fil.pt
Eyeball the contemporary art of 60 galleries from Portugal and yonder at this mammoth fair, held at Feira Internacional de Lisboa (p96) in Parque das Nações. Tots get creative at Art Kids.

Dia de São Martinho
Scoff roasted chestnuts and get smashed on fruity *água-pé* (young wine) on 11 November in celebration of St Martin.

DECEMBER

Lisbon Marathon
www.lisbon-marathon.com
Lisbon's pre-Yuletide dash from Praça do Comércio to Belém offers fleeting glimpses of icons like Ponte 25 de Abril and Torre de Belém.

New Year's Eve
Gobble 12 grapes as clocks strike midnight and join revellers at Torre de Belém to ring in the New Year with riverside fireworks, free concerts and DJs.

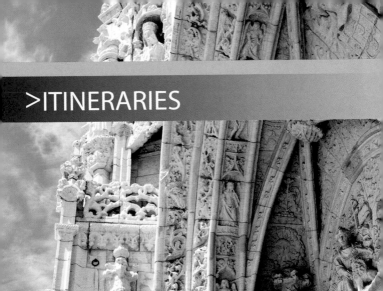

>ITINERARIES

The beauty is in the detail – the exquisite Manueline façade of Mosteiro dos Jerónimos (p80)

ITINERARIES

Don't let Lisbon's seven hills dwarf you. Whether unravelling Alfama's Moorish maze, combing Baixa's boutiques or reliving nautical adventures in time capsule Belém, this city is made for serendipitous wandering. When temperatures soar, you can cool off in Sintra's enchanted forests or with an Atlantic paddle and still make it back in time for some Bairro Alto bar-hopping.

DAY ONE

Hitch an early-morning ride on tram 28 (p15) for a rattle 'n' roll spin of Lisbon's trophy sights. Snap top-of-Lisbon views from the precipitous Moorish ramparts of Castelo de São Jorge (p65), then saunter down to Largo das Portas do Sol for *bica* (espresso) and vistas to the cobalt Rio Tejo. Explore Alfama's labyrinthine lanes of billowing laundry, sun-dappled squares and gabbling locals. Porta d'Alfama (p72) is ideal for a sardine feast on the cobbles, along with impromptu fado. Glimpse honey-bricked Sé cathedral (p69) en route to Rua Augusta (p52) for high-street shopping. At dusk, get your *ginjinha* (cherry brandy) fix at closet-sized A Ginjinha (p60). Dine in style at Olivier (p46), before sundowners at Noobai (p49) as Lisbon starts to twinkle.

DAY TWO

Wake up over oven-warm, cinnamon-dusted *pastéis de nata* (custard tarts) at vaulted Antiga Confeitaria de Belém (p82). Now beat the crowds to the fantastical Manueline cloisters of Unesco-listed Mosteiro dos Jerónimos (p80). Shadow the river to shipshape Padrão dos Descobrimentos (p81) and whimsical fortress Torre de Belém (p81), flashbacks to Portugal's Age of Discovery. Eyeball Warhol and Picasso originals for free at sleek Museu Colecção Berardo (p80), then refuel over salads and fresh OJ at Cafeteria Quadrante (p84) over the road. Spend a lazy afternoon strolling palm-dotted Jardim da Estrela (p112) and contemplating the porcelain-white baroque dome of Basílica da Estrela (p112). After dark, grab some sushi at John Malkovich's spacey restaurant Bica do Sapato (p70), then shuffle over to dockside clubbing temple Lux (p75) for superstar DJs spinning house.

Top Thought-provoking modern art on display at Museu Colecção Berardo (p80), Centro Cultural de Belém **Bottom** Cap off your magical Lisbon day by catching some live music in one of the city's funky bars

DAY THREE

If you're not nursing a *ressaca* (hangover), board the metro to Gare do Oriente (p90), Santiago Calatrava's crystalline wonder built for Expo '98. Enjoy tantalising river glimpses through the frangipani in colonial-themed Jardim Garcia de Orta (p90) en route to Europe's longest bridge – 17.2km Ponte Vasco da Gama (p92). Chomp fresh fish on the terrace at Atanvá (p94), then bid *bom dia* to the sharks and sea otters at the mother of all aquariums, Oceanário (p91). Head back into town to shop along Parisian-style boulevard Avenida da Liberdade (p98) or get your art fix at Museu Calouste Gulbenkian (p101), showcasing Rodin's eternal *Spring Kiss*. Book a table at glass-fronted Eleven (p103) for mesmeric views and Michelin-starred cuisine.

COOL SUMMER

When Lisbon starts to swelter, take the train to Sintra (p124) for a cool hike through ferny, boulder-speckled woodlands. Hide in the fairy-tale grottoes of Quinta da Regaleira (p124) and seek the snaking fortifications of Castelo dos Mouros (p125). Before leaving, snap the iconic chimneys of Unesco-listed Palácio Nacional de Sintra (p124). If you'd rather get sandy, nip across to Cascais (p126) for a tingling Atlantic dip, beach lounging and lip-smacking seafood by the waterfront. As the sun sinks into the ocean, head back to Lisbon refreshed and ready for alfresco bites and ice-cold beers on the streets of Bairro Alto (p36).

FOR FREE

Lisbon's a terrific city for euro-pinchers, as its biggest thrills are outdoors – from getting high on views from its leafy *miradouros* (viewpoints; p20) to drinking in the medieval spirit of Alfama (p64) or the hubbub of Rossio (p55). Cultural freebies you cry? Admire Romanesque Sé cathedral (p69), Roman theatre ruins at Museu do Teatro Romano (p68) and the candy-striped dome of neoclassical Basílica da Estrela (p112). If it's Sunday morning, see Rembrandt masterpieces gratis at Museu Calouste Gulbenkian (p101) before a languid stroll through manicured Parque Eduardo VII (p101). Toast your good fortune tasting citrusy Alentejo and bold Douro wines for nothing at ViniPortugal (p61) on arcaded Praça do Comércio (p54). July brings a riot of colour, music and acrobatics to free street festival BaixAnima (p25).

FORWARD PLANNING

Two months before you go Brush up your Portuguese by clicking onto www.bbc.co.uk/languages or www.easyportuguese.com. Bag hard-to-get tickets for summertime bashes like Super Bock Super Rock (p26).

One month before you go Make reservations for top tables such as Olivier (p46) and Michelin-starred Eleven (p103). Get tickets for cutting-edge performing arts at Centro Cultural de Belém (p86) and Teatro Nacional de São Carlos (p50).

Two weeks before you go Scan www.visitlisboa.com or http://timeout.sapo.pt for upcoming event details. Snag tickets for a football match at Estádio da Luz (p108).

A few days before you go Book top-notch fado at Clube de Fado (p73) or dolphin-watching tours in Setúbal (p123). Check the websites of Music Box (p50) and Cabaret Maxime (p107) for gigs, or Lux (p75) for pulsating club nights.

LISBON SHOPATHON

Start with a mooch around well-heeled Chiado for catwalk couture at Ana Salazar (p42) and so-soft kid gloves at art-deco Luvaria Ulisses (p42). Find fairy-tale wefts at Story Tailors (p44) and tongue-in-cheek souvenirs at The Wrong Shop (p44). For a lingering taste of Lisbon, groom Baixa's streets for (shippable) wines at Napoleão (p56), pungent cheeses at ye olde Manuel Tavares (p56) and retro-wrapped sardines at Conserveira de Lisboa (p55). Revive shopping-weary feet over sticky pastries at Confeitaria Nacional (p58). Then bag yourself some designs by innovative Lisbon creatives like Jorge Moita at Fabrico Infinito (p42). As dusk approaches, go boho in Bairro Alto hunting for vintage garb at glitterbugs like Agência 117 (p41) and Happy Days (p42), or funk up your feet with retro Adidas at Sneakers Delight (p44).

Pedestrianised Rua Augusta, from Praça do Comércio to Praça da Figueira, is quintessential central Lisbon

NEIGHBOURHOODS

Moorish ramparts, throbbing nightlife and crystalline high-rises – Lisbon packs in a different personality for each of its seven hills, blankly refusing to dance to a globalised tune.

At its heart is literary Chiado, harbouring pavement cafes, chichi boutiques and the architectural enigma of Convento do Carmo. Its hyperactive neighbour, Bairro Alto, is an electric mix of vintage fashion, appetising bistros and all-night bars. Revellers drink on the street, hash-peddlers avoid the law and everyone dodges the passionately driven taxis. Its microzones include Cais do Sodré for sweaty gigs, gay-friendly Príncipe Real and boho hangout Santa Catarina.

Edging east you reach the gridlike Baixa, Marquês de Pombal's 18th-century, postearthquake brainchild. Praça do Comércio evokes the heyday of Portuguese royalty with grand arcades, while pedestrianised Rua Augusta throngs with bag-toting shoppers and buskers. Moving north, Rossio is all theatrical plazas and microscopic *ginjinha* (cherry brandy) bars.

Nudging Baixa is working-class Alfama, a labyrinth of winding alleys and sun-dappled squares. Vintage trams rattle, fish sizzles, laundry flaps and neighbours gabble to the backbeat of traditional fado. Its key sights are fortresslike Sé cathedral and hilltop Castelo de São Jorge. Further north, Graça unravels giddy *miradouros* (viewpoints), the hubbub of Feira da Ladra flea market, and Igreja de São Vicente da Fora's peaceful cloisters.

A short tram ride west of the centre takes you to Belém, an Age of Discovery time capsule where Manueline treasures like Mosteiro dos Jerónimos demand exploration. A metro ride north brings you to Parque das Nações, catapulting you into the 21st century with cutting-edge architecture, public art and underwater marvel Oceanário.

North of Baixa, bustling Marquês de Pombal, Rato and Saldanha dish up foodie haunts like Michelin-starred Eleven, designer shopping on Avenida da Liberdade and top-drawer galleries including Museu Calouste Gulbenkian. Go west of Bairro Alto to explore affluent Estrela and Lapa for tranquil parks, boutique hotels and high culture. Down by the river, where Ponte 25 de Abril rumbles, Doca de Alcântara's warehouses offer high-octane clubbing.

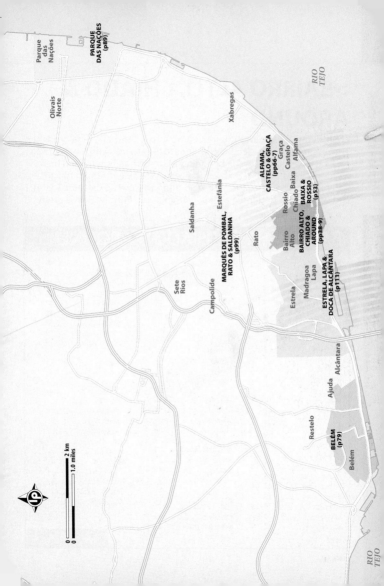

0   2 km
0   1.0 miles

Parque das Nações

PARQUE
DAS NAÇÕES
(p99)

Olivais Norte

RIO TEJO

Xabregas

Estefânia

ALFAMA,
CASTELO & GRAÇA
(pp66-7)
Graça
Castelo
Alfama

Saldanha

Rossio
Chiado Baixa

BAIRRO ALTO,
CHIADO &
AROUND
(pp38-9)

BAIXA &
ROSSIO
(p53)

MARQUÊS DE POMBAL,
RATO & SALDANHA
(p99)

Rato

Bairro
Alto

Campolide

Sete
Rios

Estrela

Madragoa
Lapa

ESTRELA, LAPA &
DOCA DE ALCÂNTARA
(p111)

RIO TEJO

Alcântara

Ajuda

Restelo

BELÉM
(p79)

Belém

RIO TEJO

>BAIRRO ALTO, CHIADO & AROUND

Loud, flirtatious and attitude-free, Bairro Alto is Lisbon's eternal student. The rat's maze of cobbled lanes springs to life at dusk, with hippie chicks seeking '60s glitz in vintage boutiques playing scratchy vinyl and merry amigos spilling out of retro bars. The party vibe extends south to Santa Catarina for cityscapes and indie bars, and Rua Nova do Carvalho for hot and sweaty gigs under the arches. Further north, Príncipe Real is pretty

BAIRRO ALTO, CHIADO & AROUND

Please see over for map

and pink. Lisbon's creative pulse, hedonist and dirtiest dancer – nobody puts Bairro in a corner.

Heading east via Praça Luís de Camões, Chiado is Bairro Alto's more graceful, grown-up sister, where grand 18th-century edifices shelter theatres, designer boutiques and old-world cafes. Art junkies get their Rodin fix at Museu do Chiado, while architecture buffs marvel at the skeletal arches of Convento do Carmo. Apparently, the district is named after poet António Ribeiro aka *chiado* (squeak). Its literary soul lives on.

SEE

☢ CONVENTO DO CARMO
☎ 213 478 629; Largo do Carmo; adult/under 14yr/concession €2.50/free/1.50; ⏱ 10am-6pm Apr-Sep, 10am-5pm Oct-Mar; Ⓜ Baixa-Chiado

Rising like a vision above Lisbon, this mesmerising Gothic convent was all but devoured by the 1755 earthquake; all that remains are the wishbones of its lofty arches, pillars and flying buttresses. Its archaeology museum reveals gems from baroque *azulejos* (tiles) to a trio of mummies – one battered Egyptian and two gruesome 16th-century Peruvians.

☢ ELEVADOR DA BICA
Rua de São Paulo; €1.35; ⏱ 7am-9pm Mon-Sat, 9am-9pm Sun; Ⓜ Cais do Sodré

Arthritically creaking up the chasmlike Rua da Bica de Duarte Belo, this iconic yellow funicular is a flashback to the late 19th century. Hitch a ride to save your legs and enjoy fleeting glimpses of the Rio Tejo and pastel-hued houses.

☢ IGREJA DE SÃO ROQUE
☎ 213 235 381; Largo Trindade Coelho; admission free; ⏱ 8.30am-5pm; Ⓜ Rossio

Plain on the outside, dazzling on the inside, this Jesuit gem hides Florentine *azulejos* and the jewel-box Capela de São João

Sunshine and solitude at Convento do Carmo

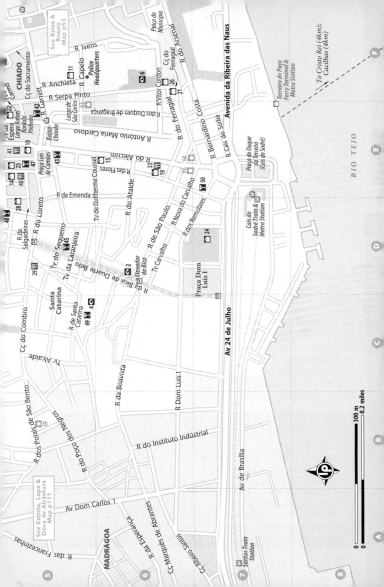

Baptista, an 18th-century chapel of amethyst, lapis lazuli and Carrara marble. Its mosaics depicting St John the Baptist's life are as intricate as oil paintings.

◉ MIRADOURO DE SANTA CATARINA
Rua de Santa Catarina; ⏲ 24hr; ▥ Elevador da Bica
Guitar-strumming teens, pot-smoking students, penniless artists…all sorts convene at this viewpoint, affording sweeping views to the river and Ponte 25 de Abril. Look for the scowling Adamastor, poet Luís de Camões' mythological sea phantom. For more information, see p20

◉ MIRADOURO DE SÃO PEDRO DE ALCÂNTARA
Rua São Pedro de Alcântara; ⏲ 24hr; Ⓜ Restauradores
Vintage funicular Elevador da Glória (p157) creaks up to this hilltop viewpoint, where Lisbon

WORTH THE TRIP
Hankering for that perfect shot of Lisbon? Take the breezy commuter ferry from Terreiro do Paço Ferry Terminal to **Cristo Rei** (☎ 212 751 000; www.cristo-rei.com; Alto do Pragal, Almada; adult/concession €4/2; ⏲ 9.30am-6pm; ▣ Cacilhas, ▣ 101). The spitting image of Rio de Janeiro's *Christ the Redeemer*, the 110m-high Jesus statue was erected in 1959 to thank God for sparing Portugal from WWII horrors. A lift whizzes up to an 82m platform affording breathtaking vistas over Lisbon. Nip into the gift shop for quality kitsch such as a Day-Glo Jesus statue for the mantelpiece.

spreads out like a patchwork before you, revealing shutterbug favourites like fortified Castelo de São Jorge. Rest beside the fountains and Greek busts.

◉ MUSEU DO CHIADO
☎ 213 432 148; www.museudochiado
-ipmuseus.pt; Rua Serpa Pinto 4; adult/

SQUARE DEAL
Extending north of Bairro Alto, Príncipe Real is home to some of Lisbon's loveliest squares, ideal for a picnic or a crowd-free stroll. Our favourite pockets of greenery:
Praça do Príncipe Real This palm-fringed plaza is shaded by a giant cedar tree. It's popular with grizzled card players by day and gay cruisers by night. There's a kids' playground and a cafe with alfresco seating.
Praça das Flores A romantic, leafy square with cobblestones, fountains and enough doggie-do to make a Parisian proud.
Praça da Alegria Swooping palms and banyan trees shade this tranquil square, a magnet for stroller-pushing parents. Keep an eye out for the bronze bust of 19th-century painter Alfredo Keil.

under 14yr/concession €4/free/2.50, 10am-2pm Sun free; ⏰ 10am-6pm Tue-Sun; Ⓜ Baixa-Chiado
In the atmospheric vaults of a former convent, this contemporary gallery showcases 19th- and 20th-century works. Crowd-pullers include Rodin and Jorge Vieira originals, Tomas Costa's euphoric *Dançarino* (1888) and António Teixeira's misty nightscape *Nocturno* (1910). Revive art-weary eyes in the garden cafe.

🛍 SHOP
High-street stores cluster on elegant Rua do Carmo, while Bairro Alto's narrow lanes harbour indie boutiques brimming with vintage garb and clubwear.

🏠 A CARIOCA *Gourmet Food*
☎ 213 420 377; Rua da Misericórdia 9; ⏰ 9am-7pm Mon-Fri, 1-7pm Sat; Ⓜ Baixa-Chiado
Get your caffeine fix at this mirrored art-deco store, a blast from the 1920s with old-fashioned service, brass fittings and an antique coffee roaster. Home-roasted blends and chocolates are lovingly wrapped in green paper.

🏠 A VIDA PORTUGUESA
Gifts & Souvenirs
☎ 213 465 073; Rua Anchieta 11; ⏰ 10am-8pm Mon-Sat; Ⓜ Baixa-Chiado

This vaulted emporium catapults you back 100 years with nostalgic Portuguese products from lime-oil soap to retro-packaged Tricona sardines and Bordallo Pinheiro porcelain swallows.

🏠 AGÊNCIA 117
Vintage Fashion
☎ 213 461 270; Rua do Norte 117; ⏰ 2pm-midnight; Ⓜ Baixa-Chiado
Bad hair day? *Nothing* to wear? Kit yourself out with jellybean-bright jersey dresses, Miss Sixty garb or tartan wellies before letting on-site hairdresser Patricia loose on your locks. Check out the fuzzy velvet crucifix!

🏠 EL DORADO *Vintage Fashion*
☎ 213 423 935; Rua do Norte 23; ⏰ 2-8pm Mon-Sat; Ⓜ Baixa-Chiado
Pencil skirts, psychedelic shirts and glitzy platforms race you back to the '60s and '70s at El Dorado. Gramophone classics play as you shop for vintage clobber and clubwear.

🏠 FÁBRICA SANT'ANNA
Ceramics
☎ 213 422 537; www.fabrica-santanna.com; Rua do Alecrim 95; ⏰ 9.30am-7pm Mon-Sat; Ⓜ Baixa-Chiado
On the tiles since 1741, Fábrica Sant'Anna handmakes and paints beautiful *azulejos*. For the lowdown, see p115.

🏠 FABRICO INFINITO *Design*
☎ 212 467 629; Rua Dom Pedro V 74A;
🕐 10am-7pm Mon-Fri; 🚠 Elevador
da Glória

Once a coach house, this light-flooded gallery presents the innovative designs of Portuguese and Brazilian creatives. The mantra: recycled meets luxury. Standouts include Marcela Brunken's born-again chandeliers and La.Ga bags by Jorge Moita (see opposite).

🏠 HAPPY DAYS *Vintage Fashion*
☎ 213 421 015; Rua do Norte 60; 🕐 1-10pm Mon-Sat; Ⓜ Baixa-Chiado

You half expect The Fonz to swagger into this '50s and '60s playground. Glitterbugs love the bauble necklaces, FLY London footwear and sequinned clutch bags.

🏠 KINKY STORE
Fashion & Accessories
☎ 968 452 041; Rua das Flores 24;
🕐 noon-8pm Mon-Fri, noon-7pm Sat;
Ⓜ Cais do Sodré

This erotica temple lures with lacy lingerie, skimpy bikinis and everything discerning divas crave – from pleasure feathers to 'bad ex' voodoo dolls.

🏠 LOUIE LOUIE *Music*
☎ 213 472 232; Rua Nova da Trindade 8; 🕐 11am-8pm Mon-Sat, 3-8pm Sun; Ⓜ Baixa-Chiado

Groove is in the heart of this DJ den, stocking secondhand vinyl and the latest house, dance and electronica.

🏠 LUVARIA ULISSES
Fashion & Accessories
☎ 213 420 295; Rua do Carmo 87A;
🕐 10am-7pm Mon-Sat; Ⓜ Baixa-Chiado

One customer at a time please… Squeeze into this art-deco gem for baby-soft kid gloves in kaleidoscopic shades.

🏠 MERCADO DA RIBEIRA
Market
☎ 210 312 600; Avenida 24 de Julho; 6am-2pm Mon-Sat; Ⓜ Cais do Sodré

BIRDS OF A FEATHER... COUTURE

Meet Lisbon's trio of catwalk fairies, revamping wardrobes with a flick of their designer wands:
Ana Salazar (☎ 213 472 289; www.anasalazar.pt; Rua do Carmo 87; 🕐 10am-7pm Mon-Sat;
Ⓜ Baixa-Chiado) Ana's virginal white flagship boutique is smack in the heart of Chiado. Sassy and feminine, her collections reveal a passion for stretch fabrics, bold prints and earthy hues.
Fátima Lopes (☎ 213 240 545; Rua da Atalaia 36; 🕐 10am-8pm Tue-Fri, 11.30am-8pm
Sat; Ⓜ Baixa-Chiado) Fátima's Latin-twist designs are figure hugging and bold – from expertly cut suits to scarlet satin ball gowns, itsy-glitzy prom dresses to electric-blue minis.
Lena Aires (☎ 213 461 815; Rua da Atalaia 96; 🕐 2pm-midnight Mon-Sat; Ⓜ Baixa-Chiado) You'll find Lena's citrus-bright, soft and playful staples at this Bairro Alto boutique.

Jorge Moita
La.Ga bag designer, Krvkurva (www.krvkurva.org) director and believer that 'to love is not an option'

Tell us about your award-winning La.Ga bags La.Ga bags are made from high-density Tyvek, a water- and radioactivity-resistant material. They're recyclable, weigh 40g and carry up to 55kg. **What's the concept?** That style can be sustainable and conscientious. **We hear they're jail-made** I'm cooperating with Tires women's prison, who represent the human face of my design. I love the inmates' honesty; they'll tell you 'this is shit' or 'it's great, I'm going to fake it when I get out'. **How does Lisbon inspire you?** Lisa [grins] is the Havana of Europe with its light, decadence and brightly coloured buildings. Here life is intuitive and real. **Where do you take time out?** I have coffee at Mar Adentro (p46) or wandering the streets of Alfama (p64).

Find picnic goodies at Lisbon's premier food market. Stalls are piled high with edibles including glossy fruit, silvery sardines and crusty loaves.

⬚ SNEAKERS DELIGHT
Fashion & Accessories
☎ 213 479 976; Rua do Norte 30;
Ⓜ Baixa-Chiado

Hipsters sneak their feet into limited edition Adidas trainers at this crayon-bright store. French artist Skwak's ogres and monsters beam down from the walls.

⬚ STORY TAILORS
Fashion & Accessories
☎ 213 432 306; Calçada do Ferragial 8;
🕐 10.30am-8pm; Ⓜ Baixa-Chiado

This enchanted forest of fashion, bedecked with gnarled wood dressers and chandeliers, is the hunting ground of Lisbon-based designers Luís and João. Their fairy-tales are floaty creations with polka dots, gingham and ruffles.

⬚ THE LOSER PROJECT
Fashion & Accessories
☎ 213 421 861; www.theloserproject
.com, Rua do Ferragial 1; 🕐 2-7pm Mon-Fri, 11am-4.30pm Sat; Ⓜ Baixa-Chiado

Gays and metrosexuals go gaga for Rui Duarte's designer threads, patent leather shoes and gold leather bags at this ubercool Chiado boutique.

⬚ THE WRONG SHOP
Gifts & Souvenirs
☎ 213 433 197; www.thewrongshop
.com; Calçada do Sacramento 25;
🕐 11am-8pm Mon-Fri, 11am-10pm Sat;
Ⓜ Baixa-Chiado

Gets it so right with chuckle-worthy gifts from blank-paged books Pessoa never wrote to 'beware of the rooster' cockerels and ever-so-friendly flycatchers.

⬚ ZED'S DAD
Fashion & Accessories
Rua da Barroca 7; 🕐 noon-8pm Mon-Wed, noon-midnight Thu-Fri, 4-8pm Sat;
Ⓜ Baixa-Chiado

Exposed stone and lightning-bolt mirrors provide a backdrop for German style-princess Nicole's retro patterns, bold '70s-style shirts and new-age lurex tops.

🍴 EAT

Late-night nibblers graze Bairro Alto's streets, peppered with hole-in-the-wall bistros serving everything from Med-style tapas to zebra steaks with *caipirinha* cocktails and a side order of cool.

🍴 A CAMPONESA
Portuguese   €€
☎ 213 464 791; Rua Marechal Saldanha 23; 🕐 12.30-3pm & 7.30-11pm Mon-Fri, dinner only Sat; Ⓜ Baixa-Chiado; Ⓥ

This sunny bistro is a favourite with Santa Catarina hipsters who lap up its arty vibe, jazzy music and home-grown flavours like plump Algarve oysters. Nice touch: tables filled with beach snapshots.

🍴 CERVEJARIA TRINDADE
Portuguese €€

☎ 213 423 506; Rua Nova da Trindade 20C; 🕑 9am-2am; Ⓜ Baixa-Chiado

Sure it's touristy, but this vaulted 13th-century monastery-turned-beer hall is still a must for its foaming beer and nonstop buzz. Quaffing clerics peer down from the tiles, as you slurp and burp feasting on lobster stew or humungous steaks.

🍴 EL GORDO II *Tapas* €€

☎ 213 426 372; Travessa dos Fiéis de Deus 28; 🕑 5pm-2am Tue-Sun; Ⓜ Baixa-Chiado

Stylish yet relaxed, Lisbon's 'fat boy two' draws alfresco diners to its cobbled steps. Lanterns cast a glow over starry-eyed couples polishing off bottles of *tinto* (red wine) and appetising tapas. Try the superb cod pastries and pimento peppers.

🍴 LISBOA Á NOITE
Portuguese €€€

☎ 213 468 557; Rua das Gáveas 69; 🕑 7.30pm-midnight Mon-Thu, 7.30pm-1am Fri & Sat; Ⓜ Baixa-Chiado

Little miss popular, Lisboa á Noite sets the scene with orange-and-

Traditional *azulejos* (tiles) and *cerveja* (beer) enjoyed in old-school surrounds at Cervejaria Trindade

white hues, soft lighting and night shots of Lisbon. The seasonally inspired menu is big on fish; the Algarve clams with octopus are superb.

🍴 LOURO & SAL
Mediterranean   €€
☎ 213 476 275; Rua da Atalaia 53; 🕒 7.30pm-midnight; Ⓜ Baixa-Chiado
Elbow-to-elbow tables, funky jazz and smiley staff create a warm feel in this bistro. Tantalising whiffs of garlic drift from the kitchen, where chefs rustle up Med-style soul food like sole ratatouille and game sausage with roast vegetables.

🍴 MAR ADENTRO *Cafe*   €
☎ 213 469 158; Rua do Alecrim 35; 🕒 10am-11pm Sun-Thu, 1pm-midnight Fri & Sat; Ⓜ Cais do Sodré
Gay-friendly Mar Adentro is king of industrial cool, sporting a razor-sharp concrete and stainless-steel design. Creative types flock here for breakfast, scrummy sandwiches (try feta, red pepper and olive) and free wi-fi.

🍴 NOOD *Sushi*   €
☎ 213 474 141; Largo Rafael Bordalo Pinheiro 20 🕒 noon-midnight Sun-Thu, noon-2am Fri & Sat; Ⓜ Baixa-Chiado
Lisbon's sushi hounds queue to snag a table at this ultraslick Japanese newcomer. Think chilli-

red walls, communal tables and wok-fresh noodles paired with fresh sushi, yakitori or sashimi. No reservations.

🍴 O BARRIGAS *Portuguese* €€
☎ 213 471 220; Travessa da Queimada 31; 🕒 7pm-1am Thu-Tue; Ⓜ Baixa-Chiado; Ⓥ
Snuggle up in this intimate, low-lit nosh spot. The name means 'the bellies' – precisely what you'll be nursing after delicacies such as fluffy *bacalhau espiritual* (salt-cod soufflé).

🍴 OLIVIER *Mediterranean* €€€
☎ 213 431 405; www.restaurante-oli vier.com; Rua do Teixeira 35; 🕒 8pm-1am Mon-Sat; Ⓜ Baixa-Chiado
The first of Lisbon masterchef Olivier da Costa's culinary triplets, this place is cosy with low ceilings, dark wood and a warm welcome from Nathalie. The tasting menu strikes perfect balance with flavours like thinly sliced octopus carpaccio and *pata negra* (cured ham) with mango chutney. See the interview on p105.

🍴 PAP'AÇORDA
Portuguese   €€€
☎ 213 464 811; Rua da Atalaia 57; 🕒 noon-2pm & 8-11.30pm Tue-Sat; Ⓜ Baixa-Chiado
Moët, sweetie? With pink-champagne walls and crystal chande-

liers, Pap'Açorda is way too sexy for Bairro. Right Said Fred lookalikes (think tall, bald, camp) bring fishy treats to the table. The must-eat is *açorda*, a garlicky bread and shell-fish stew served in a clay pot.

🍴 PASTELARIA SÃO ROQUE
Pastelaria   €
☎ 213 224 358; Rua Dom Pedro V 57;
🕑 7am-7.30pm; Ⓜ Restauradores
An opera house of a cake shop, this mirrored, oval confection drips with exquisite *azulejos* and gold flourishes. Take a pew for butter-rich rock cakes and *pastéis de nata* (custard tarts).

🍴 ROYALE CAFÉ *Cafe*   €
☎ 213 469 125; Largo Rafael Bordalo Pinheiro 29; 🕑 10am-midnight Mon-Sat, 10am-8pm Sun; Ⓜ Baixa-Chiado; Ⓥ
Yummy mummies and media types adore this chichi cafe with henna-hued walls and glam light-ing. Create your own sandwiches with fillings like Azores cheese and onion chorizo. The pink-pep-percorn tartines and papaya-mint milkshakes are divine. When the sun's out, sit in the vine-clad courtyard.

🍴 SUL *International*   €€
☎ 213 462 449; Rua do Norte 13;
🕑 noon-2am Tue-Sun; Ⓜ Baixa-Chiado
Sizzling Uruguay beef in honey-mustard sauce lures Lisboetas to

this gallery-style Bairro Alto haunt, illuminated by ostrich-egg lamps. In the mood for something more exotic? Order the zebra steak.

🍴 TAVARES RICO
Portuguese   €€€
☎ 213 421 112; Rua da Misericórdia 37;
🕑 12.30-2.30pm & 7.30-11pm Tue-Sat;
Ⓜ Baixa-Chiado
The all-gold, chandelier-lit opulence of this 18th-century restaurant would make a Viennese ballroom look shabby. Chef José Avillez shines, too, with beautifully cooked and artfully presented Portuguese flavours such as saffron-poached sea bass with Algarve clams.

🍸 DRINK
Bairro Alto's warren of lanes screams 'bar crawl' and you'll find plenty of action around Rua da Atalaia, Rua do Norte and Rua da Bica de Duarte Belo. See p13 for DIY party tips.

🍸 A BRASILEIRA *Cafe*
☎ 213 469 547; Rua Garrett 120-122;
🕑 8am-2am; Ⓜ Baixa-Chiado
Art deco in overdrive with gilt swirls, bottle-green panelling and theatrical mirrors, A Brasileira has been a Lisbon institution since 1905. Sip a *bica* (espresso) on the terrace next to poet Fernando Pessoa immortalised in bronze.

NAME GAME
Next time you want to impress Lisboetas, tell them the meaning of *bica*, which takes its name from the 1905 catchphrase of A Brasileira: *beba isto com açúcar* (drink this with sugar). It was a first attempt to lure clients to drink espresso and, judging by the jam-packed tables at the cafe today, it worked.

Buskers add a lively twist in the evening.

Y BAIRRO ALTO HOTEL
Lounge Bar
☎ 213 408 288; Praça Luís de Camões 2; ⊙ 12.30pm-midnight; Ⓜ Baixa-Chiado
A Ferrero Rocher–gold lift zooms up to Bairro Alto Hotel's vertigo-inducing terrace; a fine place for champagne-slurping and hobnobbing as Lisbon starts to twinkle.

Y BEDROOM *Lounge Bar*
☎ 213 463 028; Rua do Norte 86; ⊙ 9pm-3am Wed-Sat; Ⓜ Baixa-Chiado
Shimmery gold wallpaper, chandeliers and lounge beds draw 20-something hipsters here. Leave sleeping to the beauties and hit the dance floor, where DJs spin house with an electro twist.

Y BICAENSE *Bar*
☎ 210 156 040; Rua da Bica de Duarte Belo 42; ⊙ 12.30-3pm & 8pm-2am Mon-Sat; 🚃 Elevador da Bica

Indie kids are smitten with this Santa Catarina hotspot, crammed with retro radios and jump-on-me-now beanbags. Gigs and DJs spinning house anthems psych up the preclubbing crowd.

Y CINCO LOUNGE *Cocktail Bar*
☎ 213 424 033; Rua Ruben António Leitão 17; ⊙ 9pm-2am Tue-Sat; Ⓜ Restauradores
Award-winning mixologist Dave Palethorpe has shaken London, NYC and now Lisbon. Hitchhike his cocktail galaxy: from Singapore Slings to Milli Vanillis (hazelnut-vanilla mojitos) and Bloody Shames (vodka-free Bloody Marys). This relaxed lounge is for sipping and conversing – think chocolate sofas, candles and a kiss of gold.

Y GINJINHA DAS GÁVEAS
Ginjinha Bar
Rua das Gáveas 17A; ⊙ 9am-3am Mon-Sat; Ⓜ Baixa-Chiado
Eager to meet young Lisboetas and travellers? Lively, fun and cheap (€1 for a *ginjinha* or beer), this pint-sized bar is the place.

Y MAJONG *Bar*
☎ 213 421 039; Rua da Atalaia 3; ⊙ 9.30pm-4am; Ⓜ Baixa-Chiado
Majong is Bairro Alto's gay-friendly cabbage patch kid, with pak-choi lights, scarlet walls and old-school scruffiness. Mojitos flow as DJs play minimalist techno, rock and reggae.

☕ NOOBAI CAFÉ *Bar*
☎ 213 465 014; www.noobaicafe.com; Miradouro de Santa Catarina; 🕐 noon-midnight; 🚋 Elevador da Bica
Noobai's a reverse magic trick: now you don't see it, now you do. Descend the steps to unravel a terrace, where views sweep from the castle to Cristo Rei. Add a dash of cool, funky jazz and zingy *caipirinhas* and – abracadabra! – one of Lisbon's best bars.

☕ O'GÍLÍNS *Irish Pub*
☎ 213 421 899; Rua dos Remolares 10; 🕐 11am-2am; Ⓜ Cais do Sodré
To be sure the best craic this side of Donegal, O'Gílíns serves Guinness and big-screen sports. Wednesday to Saturday nights are a lively affair with fiddles, singing and the odd punter jigging on the table.

☕ PAVILHÃO CHINÊS *Bar*
☎ 213 424 729; Rua Dom Pedro V 89-91; 🕐 4pm-2am Mon-Sat; 9pm-2am Sun; 🚋 Elevador da Glória
Luís Pinto Coelho's wondrous junk shop would make magpies' eyes shine with its mind-boggling collection of Venetian masks and Action Men, diving spitfires and Spanish fans. Sip port or play pool in Hofburg palace meets granny's attic surrounds. The bill might sting, but such classic kitsch doesn't come cheap.

Curiosity shop interior of Pavilhão Chinês

☕ PORTAS LARGAS *Bar*
☎ 213 466 379; Rua da Atalaia 105; 🕐 7pm-3.30am; Ⓜ Baixa-Chiado
Ye olde tavern throws open *portas largas* (big doors) to a motley crew of gays, straights and not-sures, who prop up the marble bar or spill onto the cobbles with prenightclub *caipirinhas*.

☕ SOLAR DO VINHO DO PORTO *Bar*
☎ 213 475 707; Rua São Pedro de Alcântara 45; 🕐 11am-midnight Mon-Fri, from 2pm Sat; 🚋 Elevador da Glória
Slip into something more comfortable at this beamed 18th-century mansion turned port cellar. Go

NEIGHBOURHOODS

BAIRRO ALTO, CHIADO & AROUND

vintage with spicy tawny and ruby-red tipples by the glass or bottle.

⭐ PLAY

⬚ CATACUMBAS *Live Music*
☎ 213 463 969; Travessa da Água da Flor 43; cover varies; ⏱ 10pm-4am Mon-Sat; Ⓜ Baixa-Chiado

Moodily lit and festooned with portraits of jazz legends like Miles Davis, this bluesy den is jam-packed with relaxed locals when it hosts live gigs on Thursday night.

⬚ FRÁGIL *Club*
☎ 213 469 578; www.fragil.com.pt; Rua da Atalaia 126; cover free-€10; ⏱ 11.30pm-4am Tue-Sat; Ⓜ Baixa-Chiado

Frágil has been rocking Bairro Alto for 25 years and shows no sign of waning. Small and sweaty, Manuel Reis' first love before Lux (p75) draws gays and a smattering of straights. DJs Kaspar and Rui Murka spin progressive house and electronica.

⬚ INCÓGNITO *Club*
☎ 213 908 755; Rua dos Poiais de São Bento 37; ⏱ 11pm-4am Wed-Sat; 🚌 49

Despite its pipsqueak size, no-sign Incógnito lures Santa Catarina's arbiters of style, with DJs thrashing out post-rock and alternative pop. Squeeze onto the basement

dance floor to shuffle or join cocktail sippers in the loft bar.

⬚ JAMAICA *Club*
☎ 213 421 859; Rua Nova do Carvalho 8; cover €2; ⏱ 11pm-4am; Ⓜ Cais do Sodré

OK, so most dancing on this street involves laps, but not in Jamaica, man. A crowd as mixed as M&Ms – gay, straight and indifferent, black and white – shake their booties to reggae (Bob *naturalmente*) and '80s grooves. Cranks up around 2am.

⬚ MUSIC BOX *Live Music*
☎ 213 473 188; www.musicboxlisboa .com; Rua Nova do Carvalho 24; cover free-€6; ⏱ 11pm-6am Mon-Sat; Ⓜ Cais do Sodré

Under the brick arches, this pulsating box is swiftly becoming Lisbon's hottest live-music club, with gigs covering the spectrum from rock and reggae to hip hop and dance. Expect top-drawer DJs and a friendly vibe.

⬚ TEATRO NACIONAL DE SÃO CARLOS *Theatre*
☎ 213 253 045; www.saocarlos.pt; Rua Serpa Pinto 9; tickets €30-70; Ⓜ Baixa-Chiado

Lisbon's opera house is a delirious gold-and-red, cherub-and-garland extravaganza built in the 1790s. Expect a first-rate repertoire of opera, ballet, theatre and classical

PRÍNCIPE PINK

From camp bars to cruisy clubs, Praça do Príncipe Real, just north of Bairro Alto, is king of Lisbon's gay and lesbian scene. Feel the pride at our pick of Príncipe's pink venues:

Bar 106 (☎ 213 427 373; Rua de São Marçal 106; ⏱ 9pm-2am) Attracts young gay men with an upbeat, preclubbing vibe and wacky events like Sunday's message party.

Bar Água No Bico (☎ 213 472 830; Rua de São Marçal 170; ⏱ 9pm-2am) Flying the rainbow flag, this cheery bar has art exhibitions, shows and music from jazz to chill out.

Bric-a-Bar (☎ 213 428 971; Rua Cecilio de Sousa 82; ⏱ 9pm-4am) Cruisy with a 'dark room' and resident DJs.

Memorial (☎ 213 968 891; Rua Gustavo de Matos Sequeira 42A; cover €5; ⏱ 11pm-4am Tue-Sun) Mainly lesbian with dance music, camp comedy and drag shows.

Trumps (☎ 213 971 059; www.trumps.pt; Rua da Imprensa Nacional 104B; cover €10; ⏱ 11.45pm-6am Tue-Sun) Lisbon's hottest gay club with cruisy corners, a sizeable dance floor and events from live music to drag.

music in the season running from mid-September to July.

⭐ **ZÉ DOS BOIS** *Live Music*
☎ 213 430 205; www.zedosbois.org;
Rua da Barroca 59; cover €6-10;
Ⓜ Baixa-Chiado

Zé dos Bois' wildly experimental line-up feeds on tomorrow's performing art and music trends. With its graffitied courtyard and threadbare sofas, the boho haunt has welcomed the likes of New York rockers Black Dice and Animal Collective to its stage.

>BAIXA & ROSSIO

Marquês de Pombal's design for life, Baixa was built ruler-straight and rock-solid above the rubble of the 1755 earthquake. Bisected by Rua Augusta, which links arcaded Praça do Comércio to Rossio, the pedestrianised grid has enough pomp, souvenir kitsch and pigeon poo to rival Trafalgar Square. But you can't help but love Baixa, admit it. For every camera-toting tourist, there's a dazzling river view; for every Barcelos cockerel, a vintage treasure.

For the hey-I'm-in-Lisbon experience, it has to be Rossio. Bask in the fountain spray, crane your neck to spy the hilltop castle and survey the action from a sunny cafe terrace. At twilight, the zone around Largo de São Domingos swirls with women in vibrant African costumes and locals sipping *ginjinha* (cherry brandy), gravity-defying skateboarders on Praça da Figueira and alternative types at grungy drinking dens like Crew Hassan.

BAIXA & ROSSIO

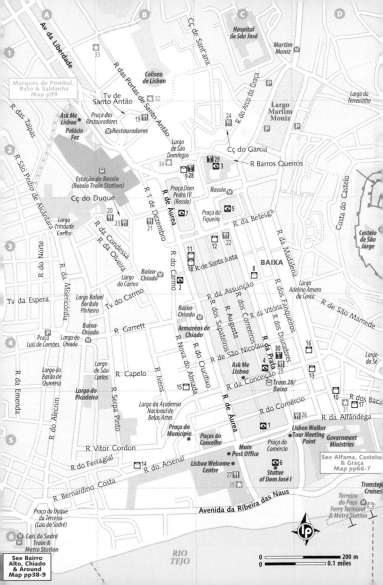

SEE

ELEVADOR DE SANTA JUSTA
☎ 213 613 054; Rua de Santa Justa;
€2.70; ☷ 7am-9pm, 7am-11pm summer;
Ⓜ Baixa-Chiado

If this wrought-iron filigree elevator seems uncannily like the Eiffel Tower, that's because it's the 1902 brainchild of Raul Mésnier, Gustav's pupil. Sticking out like the lanky kid at school, the 45m neo-Gothic lift zooms above Baixa to a rooftop cafe, affording 360-degree views over Lisbon to the river. Early birds beat the crowds, while night owls get to see it glow gold.

IGREJA DE SÃO DOMINGOS
St Dominic Church; Largo de São Domingos; admission free; ☷ 7.30am-7pm;
Ⓜ Rossio; ♿

Shattered in the 1755 earthquake and scorched by fire in 1959, it's

MAKE WAY FOR MUDE
In late 2009 Lisbon's shiny new design and fashion museum Museu do Design (MUDE) will open on Rua Augusta. Born from Francisco Capelo's outstanding collection, it will showcase contemporary creations by such design and haute-couture royalty as Le Corbusier, Frank Gehry, John Galliano, Philippe Starck and Comme des Garçons. Exact details haven't been confirmed yet, but the website www.mude.pt will keep you posted.

a miracle this church still stands. Flickering tealights illuminate gashed pillars and ethereal sculptures in its musty interior. The square is a popular hangout for Lisbon's African community.

NÚCLEO ARQUEOLÓGICO
Archaeology Centre; ☎ 213 211 700;
Rua dos Correeiros 9; tours free; ☷ tours 3-5pm Wed, 10am-noon & 3-5pm Sat;
Ⓜ Baixa-Chiado

Descend into the bowels of Lisbon at Banco Comercial Português, whose warren of subterranean tunnels is believed to be the remains of a Roman spa from the 1st century AD. Phone ahead to book.

PRAÇA DA FIGUEIRA
Ⓜ Rossio

Like its sidekick Rossio, Praça da Figueira is framed by whizzing traffic and Pombaline townhouses. At its centre rises gallant King João I, once celebrated for his 15th-century discoveries in Africa, now targeted by pigeons and gravity-defying skateboarders – that's justice for you. Take a seat at one of the pavement cafes for cake, sunshine and perfect snapshots of Castelo de São Jorge (p65).

PRAÇA DO COMÉRCIO
Ⓜ Terreiro do Paço

Marquês de Pombal's grandest design, this is a square to out-pomp

NAME DROPPING

When Marquês de Pombal let his architectural genius loose on Baixa in the aftermath of the 1755 earthquake, he named the streets after the trades that flourished there. Racing you back to those days are roads named after *sapateiros* (shoemakers), *correeiros* (saddlers), *douradores* (gilders), *fanqueiros* (cutlers), *ouro* (gold), *prata* (silver) and even *bacalhoeiros* (cod-fishing vessels). Some still reveal traces of their artisanal past; take a stroll to see what's in a name today.

them all: a whirl of 18th-century lemon-meringue edifices and arcades with vistas across the Tejo. The biggest crowd-puller is Verissimo da Costa's Arco da Vitória, a mighty triumphal arch crowned with bigwigs including explorer Vasco da Gama, which leads onto Rua Augusta.

🔘 ROSSIO
Praça Dom Pedro IV; M Rossio
Simply Rossio to locals, Praça Dom Pedro IV has 24-hour buzz. Shoe-shiners and lottery ticket sellers, hash-peddlers and office workers drift across its wavelike cobbles. And these cobbles have seen it all: with burnings and bullfights, rallies and 1974 revolution carnations (p148). Don't miss Brazil's first emperor Pedro IV high on a marble pedestal and Estação do

Rossio, a frothy neo-Manueline station with horseshoe-shaped arches and swirly turrets. Trains depart here for Sintra (p124).

🔲 SHOP

🔲 A OUTRA FACE DA LUA
Vintage Fashion
☎ 218 863 430; Rua da Assunção 22; ⏰ 10am-8pm Mon-Sat; M Rossio
Hippie chicks and Suzi Quatro wannabes hunt for vintage threads in Baixa's grooviest boutique. This dress-up box is stuffed with platforms, sequinned puffballs, corsets and retro Barbies. Take a breather over cosmic tea in the cafe.

🔲 AZEVEDO RUA
Fashion & Accessories
☎ 213 427 511; Praça Dom Pedro IV 73; ⏰ 9.30am-7pm Mon-Fri, 9.30am-1pm Sat; M Rossio
Berets and Panamas, flat caps and bonnets – Lisbon's maddest hatters have been covering bald spots since 1886. Enter this Victoriana time capsule for old-school service and everything from Ascot-worthy headwear to spiffy Fred Astaire–style canes.

🔲 CONSERVEIRA DE LISBOA
Gourmet Food
☎ 218 864 009; Rua dos Bacalhoeiros 34; ⏰ 9am-7pm Mon-Fri, 9.30am-1pm Sat; 🚋 28
How apt that in Rua dos Bacalhoeiros (cod-vessel street) lies a

store full to the gills with tinned fish. This 1930s gem has an antique till and elderly ladies busy retro-wrapping sardines, tuna and cod. Check out the pearly whites of the Tricana girl, bet she never had fish breath…

DISCOTECA AMÁLIA
Music
☎ 213 421 485; Rua de Áurea 272; ☯ 9.30am-7pm Mon-Fri, 9.30am-1pm Sat; Ⓜ Rossio
A shrine to *fadista* Amália Rodrigues, this little store lures music lovers with its excellent fado and classical collection.

MANUEL TAVARES
Gourmet Food
☎ 213 424 209; Rua da Betesga 1A; ☯ 9.30am-7.30pm Mon-Sat; Ⓜ Rossio
Come all ye faithful lovers of wine, port and waist-expanding treats. Dating to 1860, this wood-fronted store tempts with smoked hams, cheeses, *pata negra* (cured ham) and *ginjinha*.

NAPOLEÃO *Wine*
☎ 218 861 108; Rua dos Fanqueiros 70; ☯ 9.30am-8pm Mon-Sat, noon-7pm Sun; 🚋 28
This little corker fizzes with Portuguese wines from citrusy Alentejos to ruby-red Douros and ports. The

A gourmand's paradise – stocking up on essentials at Manuel Tavares

COCK-A-DOODLE-ALLEY

Rua Augusta is chock-full of kitsch shops itching for you to spend euros on pocket-sized trams, 'I love Pessoa' T-shirts, Lisbon landmark boxer shorts and, of course, our ubiquitous feathered friend Galo de Barcelos. The punk rooster with a heart pops up on tea towels, keyrings, coasters and watches; an avian all-rounder who is, as it were, Portugal's biggest souvenir cock-up. But if you think *you're* sick of the bird, spare a thought for the residents of Barcelos in northern Portugal. They've suffered years of crowing since, legend has it, a pilgrim sentenced to death for theft proved his innocence by making the little rooster *có-ró-có-có*.

family might let you have a tipple on the house. Ships worldwide.

REI DO BACALHAU
Gourmet Food

110 Rua do Arsenal, 🕑 **8am-7pm Mon-Sat;** Ⓜ **Terreiro do Paço**
At this humble 'king of cod' you can buy dried, salted *bacalhau* by the gram. And who can resist those potted cod tongues and fins? Mmmm…

SANRIO STORE
Gifts & Souvenirs

☎ **213 476 070; Rua Nova do Almada 15;** 🕑 **10am-7.30pm;** Ⓜ **Baixa-Chiado**
With a giant twinkling moggie at its entrance, this bubble-gum-pink

store makes Hello Kitty fans purr with its array of ever-so girly toys and clothing; from rose-tinted tea sets to feline bikinis.

SANTOS OFÍCIOS
Gifts & Souvenirs

☎ **218 872 031; Rua da Madalena 87;** 🕑 **10am-8pm Mon-Sat;** 🚋 **28**
If you're after Portuguese crafts, Santos has the real deal. Handmade souvenirs at this brick-vaulted store include Madeira lace, glazed earthenware, nativity scenes and *azulejos* (tiles).

SILVA & FEIJÓ *Gourmet Food*
Rua dos Bacalhoeiros 117; 🕑 **10am-1pm & 2.30-7.30pm Mon-Sat;** 🚋 **28**
Picnickers head for this wood-beamed store, crammed with goodies like sardine pâté, rye bread, herby *salsichas* (sausages) and pungent sheep's cheese from the mountains of Seia.

CLASSIC STITCH-UP

Rua da Conceição recalls an era where folk still used to darn stockings with its cluster of dark wood-panelled, closet-sized haberdasheries. Keep your beady eyes open for buttons, ribbons and threads in myriad shades as you stroll along. Our favourites include Nardo at No 62, Alexandre Bento at No 69 and Botão Dourado at No 115. This old-timer gets our vote as the Baixa's most charming street and is a breath of fresh air from the high-street crowds.

🏠 ZOTTER *Gourmet Food*
☎ 213 462 253; Rua de Santa Justa 84;
🕑 8am-7pm Mon-Sat; Ⓜ Rossio
Oops, there goes another diet! This bijou Austrian chocolatier promises to *faz te feliz* (make you happy) with bittersweet 100% cocoa bars and creamier varieties laced with flavours such as *ginjinha*, chestnut, lemon curd and – why ever not? – tofu.

🍴 EAT
Dine alfresco on Calçada do Duque's cobbled steps for views of the castle illuminated. Rua das Portas de Santo Antão harbours good-value fish bistros with pavement seating and lots of buzz.

🍴 BONJARDIM *Portuguese* €
☎ 213 424 389; Travessa de Santo Antão 11; 🕑 noon-11pm; Ⓜ Restauradores
Lisbon's hottest chicks are served spit-roasted with mounds of fries and salad at this local favourite. Grab a chair on the pavement terrace for a *frango* (chicken) feast. For extra spice, ask for piri-piri.

🍴 CAFÉ BUENOS AIRES
International €€
☎ 213 420 739; Calçada do Duque 31;
🕑 6pm-1am Mon-Sat; Ⓜ Rossio
With more swing, steam and embracing couples on weekends than a Buenos Aires tango hall, this is Rossio's hippest cafe.

Tealights flicker in the boho-style confines, where gringos polish off juicy Argentine steaks and chocolate cake with *dulce de leche* (caramelised milk). And the views from the steps? Wow.

🍴 CELEIRO *Cafe* €
☎ 213 422 463; Rua 1 de Dezembro 65;
🕑 8.30am-8pm Mon-Fri, 8.30am-7pm Sat; Ⓜ Rossio; Ⓥ
Get juiced and eat your greens at this vitamin-loaded cafe just off Rossio. The lunchtime crowds pile into Celeiro for cheap and healthy vegetarian specials like quiche and pizza.

🍴 CONFEITARIA NACIONAL
Pastelaria €
☎ 213 461 720; Praça da Figueira 18;
🕑 8am-8pm Mon-Sat; Ⓜ Rossio
If the window display of almond biscuits, macaroons and custard

CENT SAVER
Yep, many restaurants on Rua Augusta dish up mediocre and overpriced grub, but gastro salvation is close by. Just paces from the shuffling masses are quieter streets where bistros and grill houses offer more bang for your euro. Check out the cafes on Rua dos Correeiros for Portuguese staples and alfresco seating, the curry dens down Rua dos Sapateiros for a midday balti, or simply wander and see where your rumbling stomach leads you...

However will you choose? Counters stacked with sticky treats at Confeitaria Nacional

tarts doesn't lure you in, the smell of freshly roasted *bica* (espresso) will. Since 1829 this cake shop has been fattening up Lisboetas in stuccoed surrounds.

🍴 EL REI D'FRANGO
Portuguese €
☎ 213 424 066; Calçada do Duque 5; ⏱ 9am-8.30pm Mon-Sat; Ⓜ Rossio
Three words: Lisbon's best-kept secret. Grill goddesses Luciana and Carla ensure diners *roll down* Calçada do Duque's cobblestone steps after humungous salmon steaks or *febras* (pork strips) at this unassuming local haunt.

🍴 EVEREST MONTANHA
International €
☎ 218 876 428; Calçada do Garcia 15; ⏱ 11.30am-3.30pm & 7pm-midnight; Ⓥ
At this diminutive Everest, chefs reach Himalayan heights with Nepalese pakoras, gobis and smooth mango lassis. We love the flavourful lamb korma and fish curry.

🍴 FRAGOLETO *Ice Cream* €
☎ 218 877 971; Rua da Prata 74; ⏱ 9am-8pm Mon-Sat; Ⓜ Baixa-Chiado; Ⓥ
For the tastiest gelato this side of Genoa, head to pint-sized Fragoleto. Manuela Carabina whips up authentic ice cream using fresh,

seasonal fruit. Our current favourites: pistachio, green tea and wild berries.

🍴 MARTINHO DA ARCADA
Portuguese €€€

☎ 218 879 259; Praça do Comércio 37; ⏰ 8am-10pm; Ⓜ Terreiro do Paço

One-time haunt of poet Fernando Pessoa, Martinho has been a Baixa linchpin since 1782. Take a pew under the colonnade for people-watching and hearty staples like *cataplana* (seafood stew).

🍴 TERREIRO DO PAÇO
Modern Portuguese €€€

☎ 210 312 850; Praça do Comércio; ⏰ 12.30-3pm & 8-11pm Mon-Fri, dinner only Sat; Ⓜ Terreiro do Paço

This brick-vaulted, gallery-style restaurant on the square once formed part of the royal palace. Award-winning chef Vítor Sobral imaginatively interprets Portuguese cuisine – think caramelised duck with baked banana and Azores tuna with ginger soufflé.

🍸 DRINK

Rossio's microscopic *ginjinha* bars ooze atmosphere. For high-octane nightlife, work up a thirst climbing the steps to Bairro Alto.

🍸 A GINJINHA *Ginjinha Bar*
Largo de São Domingos 8; ⏰ 9am-10.30pm; Ⓜ Rossio

This shoebox-sized *ginjinha* bar has been inebriating locals since the 1840s, with Lisbon's stickiest floors to prove it. The drink's inventor, Espinheiro, keeps beady watch over the door. For more, see p16.

🍸 GINJINHA RUBI *Ginjinha Bar*
Rua Barros Queirós 27; ⏰ 7am-midnight; Ⓜ Rossio

Squeeze into this hole-in-the-wall bar to natter with locals over a *ginjinha* or three and admire the *azulejos*.

🍸 NÉCTAR WINE BAR *Wine Bar*
☎ 912 633 368; Rua dos Douradores 33; ⏰ 12.30-3pm & 6-11pm Mon-Thu, 12.30-3pm & 6pm-midnight Fri & Sat; Ⓜ Baixa-Chiado

If wine is the nectar of the gods, this bar is sacred. Funky lounge music, art-slung walls and a laid-back vibe attract young Lisboetas keen to swirl reds, whites and vintage ports. Tasting plates of octopus salad and game sausage are superb.

⭐ PLAY

⭐ BACALHOEIRO
Alternative Culture

☎ 218 864 891; 2nd fl, Rua dos Bacalhoeiros 125; membership €5; ⏰ 6pm-2am Tue-Sun, 6pm-4am Fri & Sat; 🚊 28

Bacalhoeiro is like gatecrashing a private party. Once you've coughed up the membership, you're free to enjoy alternative gigs, film screenings, salsa nights and themed parties like Intergalactic Star Wars ('80s cheese and electro). Free wi-fi.

⭐ COLISEU DOS RECREIOS
Concert Hall

☎ 213 240 580; www.coliseulisboa.com; Rua das Portas de Santo Antão 96; tickets €15-240; Ⓜ Restauradores

Lisbon's elliptical concert hall hosts top-drawer performances such as concerts, opera, theatre and dance. Stars from *fadista* Ana Moura to industrial rockers Nine Inch Nails and flamenco's enfant terrible Rafael Amargo have graced its stage.

⭐ CREW HASSAN
Alternative Culture

☎ 213 466 119; www.crewhassan.org; 1st fl, Rua das Portas de Santo Antão 159; admission free-€5; ⏲ 10pm-2am; Ⓜ Restauradores; Ⓥ

Grungy, nonconformist and anticapitalist, Crew Hassan smells like teen spirit. The grassroots coop draws alternative types who dig its graffiti, threadbare sofas, cheap veggie fare and free internet. The line-up spans flicks, exhibitions, gigs and DJs spinning music from minimalist techno to reggae.

⭐ TEATRO NACIONAL D MARIA II *Theatre*

☎ 213 250 835; www.teatro-dmaria .pt; Praça Dom Pedro IV; tickets €8-16; Ⓜ Rossio

THE DARKNESS
Nothing of Teatro Nacional D Maria II's neoclassical grandeur evokes its sinister background as Palácio dos Estaus, seat of the Portuguese Inquisition from 1540. Those found guilty of heresy, witchcraft or practising Judaism were publicly executed on Rossio or Largo de São Domingos. Though King João III, or *o Piedoso* (the Pious), launched the Inquisition in 1536, the persecution of Jews goes back further; look for the Star of David in front of Igreja de São Domingos (p54), which marks the spot of a bloody anti-Semitic massacre in 1506.

This neoclassical theatre rose like a phoenix from the ashes of Palácio dos Estaus, seat of the Portuguese Inquisition (see the boxed text on above). Underfunding means its performing arts line-up is somewhat hit and miss.

⭐ VINIPORTUGAL
Wine Tasting

☎ 213 420 690; www.viniportugal.pt; Praça do Comércio; ⏲ 11am-7pm Tue-Sat; Ⓜ Terreiro do Paço

ViniPortugal is a terrific initiative to promote Portuguese wine. In the cool, vaulted showroom, you can taste wines from grapefruity Alentejo whites to round Douros for free, and learn about their geography. Bubbly staff will help you choose and value your opinion.

WALKING TOUR
BAIXA TO CHIADO

Begin in the heart of Lisbon, **Praça do Comércio** (**1**, p54), where the thring-thring of tram bells mingles with buskers' strumming. Stroll

the cool arcades, marvel at the lemon-meringue edifices and nip into **ViniPortugal** (**2**, p61) to taste Portuguese wines for free. Next, strike a pose in front of the triumphal arch and walk through it onto buzzy **Rua Augusta** (**3**, p57), where

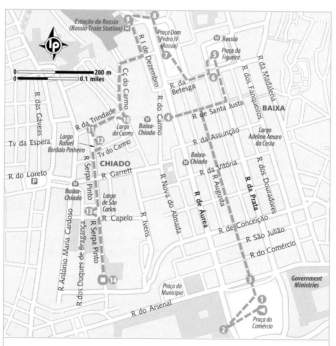

distance 4.5km **duration** Five to six hours ▶ **start** Praça do Comércio ● **end** Museu do Chiado

high-street stores and souvenir kitsch vie for your euros. Buy a cockerel, soak up the street life, then when you hit Rua de Santa Justa, look to your left and you'll spy the filigree **Elevador de Santa Justa** (**4**, p54), Lisbon's Eiffel-inspired vertical street lift, affording striking 360-degree views over the city. Done, toddle east along Rua de Santa Justa then north up Rua da Prata to **Praça da Figueira** (**5**, p54), where skateboarders cruise past Pombaline townhouses and vistas of hilltop Castelo de São Jorge give you the shutterbug. Time for morning coffee? Revive over *bica* and gooey tarts at nostalgic, 19th-century **Confeitaria Nacional** (**6**, p58). Head straight onto **Rossio** (**7**, p55) for a disorientating wander across the wavelike cobbles to see dancing fountains, the graceful columns of neoclassical **Teatro Nacional D Maria II** (**8**, p61), and the barley-twist turrets and horseshoe arches of neo-Manueline **Estação do Rossio** (**9**, p55). Go west up the steep, cobbled Calçada do Carmo to Largo do Carmo, a tranquil square where Lisboetas sip coffee

at pavement cafes, grizzled men gather to play cards and purple jacaranda trees bloom in spring. The biggest stunner here is the ethereal **Convento do Carmo** (**10**, p37), its skeletal arches and ruined pillars completely exposed to the elements. Treasures inside its museum include eerie Peruvian mummies. Now cross the square to Rua da Trindade to glimpse the 1864 trompe l'oeil *azulejos* of **Casa do Ferreira das Tabuletas** (**11**, p139), depicting goddesses and the elements. You'll soon emerge at Largo Rafael Bordalo Pinheiro, where arty haunt **Royale Café** (**12**, p47) makes a perfect lunch stop. Get creative designing your own sandwich and retreat to the vine-clad inner courtyard when the weather warms. Fortified, amble down Rua Serpa Pinto, pausing to admire the graceful arches of **Teatro Nacional de São Carlos** (**13**, p50), Chiado's elegant 18th-century opera house. Continue further down the street to one-time convent **Museu do Chiado** (**14**, p40) for a late-afternoon art fix of Rodin and Jorge Vieira originals.

>ALFAMA, CASTELO & GRAÇA

Castelo de São Jorge's colossal ramparts overshadow Alfama, Lisbon's Moorish time capsule. Wandering its steep *becos* (alleys), palm-shaded plazas and wriggling passageways will set your senses on high alert. One minute it's the play of light on candy-hued houses, the next a *miradouro* (viewpoint) overlooking a jigsaw of terracotta rooftops streaked blue by the Tejo. But what gives the prettiness a face are *alfacinhas,* the earthy locals who fill its lanes with banter, freshly washed laundry, sizzling fish and the mournful ballads of fado (traditional melancholy Portuguese song). For more, see p11.

Up north in leafy Graça, the pearly white domes of Panteão Nacional and Igreja de São Vicente da Fora punctuate the skyline, best surveyed from the giddy heights of Miradouro da Senhora do Monte. Quaintness overkill? Head down to Santa Apolónia, where John Malkovich's ultracool siblings Bica do Sapato and clubbing temple Lux offer the perfect 21st-century antidote.

ALFAMA, CASTELO & GRAÇA

⊙ SEE
Casa dos Bicos	1	C5
Castelo de São Jorge	2	C4
Igreja de São Vicente de Fora	3	E3
Largo das Portas do Sol	4	D4
Miradouro da Graça	5	D2
Miradouro da Senhora do Monte	6	C1
Miradouro de Santa Luzia	7	D4
Museu de Artes Decorativas	8	D4
Museu do Fado	9	E4
Museu do Teatro Romano	10	C4
Olisipónia	11	C3
Panteão Nacional	12	F3
Sé Cathedral	13	C5

🛍 SHOP
A Arte da Terra	14	C5
Articula	15	E4
Feira da Ladra (Thieves Market)	16	F2
Garrafeira da Sé	17	D5
Ponte Lisboa	18	C5

🍴 EAT
Bica do Sapato	19	G3
Botequim São Martinho	20	D5
Casanova	21	G3
Divinha Sedução	22	D5
Grelhador de Alfama	23	E4
O Faz Figura	24	F3
Pois Café	25	D5
Porta d'Alfama	26	D5
Restô	27	C4
Santo Antonio de Alfama	28	D4
Senhora Mãe	29	D4
Viagem de Sabores	30	C5

🍸 DRINK
Bar das Imagens	31	C4
Ginja D'Alfama	32	E4
Última Sé	33	C5

⭐ PLAY
A Baiuca	34	D4
Chapitô	35	C4
Clube de Fado	36	D5
Lux	37	G3
Mesa de Frades	38	E4
Onda Jazz	39	D5
Parreirinha de Alfama	40	E4

Please see over for map

SEE
CASA DOS BICOS
☎ 218 810 900; Rua dos Bacalhoeiros; closed to the public; 🚋 28

Once the abode of Afonso de Albuquerque, conqueror of Goa, this 16th-century confection is the architectural equivalent of a hedgehog; its spiky façade chequered with 1125 pyramid-shaped stones. Though it houses a private organisation, you can nip inside to see the remains of the old Moorish city wall if the lobby is open.

CASTELO DE SÃO JORGE
St George's Castle; ☎ 218 800 620; www.castelosaojorge.egeac.pt; adult/under 10yr/concession €5/free/2.50; ⏱ 9am-9pm Mar-Oct, 9am-6pm Nov-Feb; 🚋 28

Lording it over Lisbon, this Moorish fortress squeezes into every snapshot. These walls have seen it all: from Moors in the 9th century to Crusaders in 1147, Portuguese kings to convicts. Beat the crowds to the ramparts and pine-fringed courtyards for mesmerising views. Near the entrance, **Olisipónia** (⏱ 9am-8.30pm Mar-Oct, 9am-5.30pm Nov-Feb) whizzes through Lisbon's history, but glosses over anything unpalatable (did anyone say slave trade?).

IGREJA DE SÃO VICENTE DA FORA
☎ 218 824 400; Largo de São Vicente; adult/child €4/2; ⏱ 10am-6pm Tue-Sun; 🚋 28

Out of earshot of Lisbon's bustle, this ivory-white, 12th-century monastery was rebuilt after collapsing on worshippers in 1755's earthquake (p147). Its serene cloisters dance with elaborate blue-and-white *azulejos* (tiles). Seek out the cloaked woman holding stony vigil in the eerie mausoleum, and tiled panels of La Fontaine fables

---

GETTING HIGH ON LISBON
Alfama and Graça afford cracking views from their precipitous *miradouros* (viewpoints), each offering a slightly different perspective on Lisbon. Our favourites:
Largo das Portas do Sol An original Moorish gateway, this viewpoint is ideal for that must-have shot of Alfama's tumbledown, pastel-coloured houses.
Miradouro de Santa Luzia Centred on a trickling fountain, this bougainvillea-draped lookout overlooks Alfama's blushing rooftops.
Miradouro da Graça Young Lisboetas flock to this pine-fringed square at dusk for sundowners and sweeping vistas over central Lisbon.
Miradouro da Senhora do Monte Lisbon's highest point boasts superlative views of the castle and has a relaxed vibe.

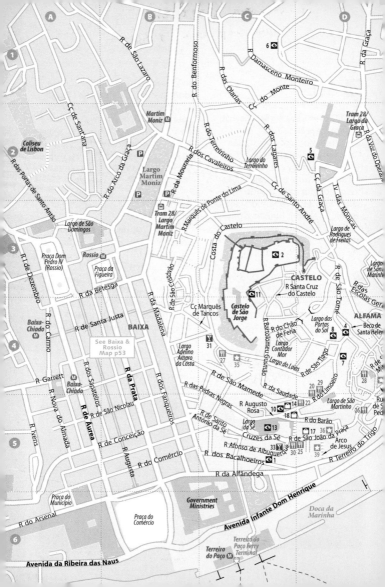

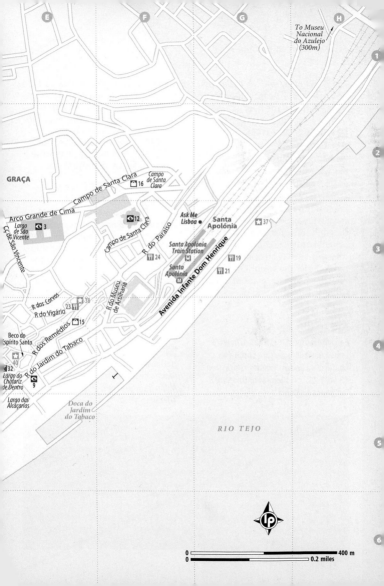

To Museu
Nacional
do Azulejo
(300m)

GRAÇA

Campo de Santa Clara

Campo
de Santa
Clara

16

Arco Grande de Cima

12

R do Paraíso

Ask Me
Lisboa

Santa
Apolónia

37

Largo
de São
Vicente

3

Cª de São Vicente

Campo de Santa Clara

Santa Apolónia
Train Station

Santa
Apolónia

19

24

21

R do Museu
de Artilharia

R dos Corvos

R do Vigário

23

38

Avenida Infante Dom Henrique

15

Beco do
Espírito Santo

R dos Remédios

40

R do Jardim do Tabaco

32

Largo do
Chafariz
de Dentro

9

Largo das
Alcaçarias

Doca do
Jardim
do Tabaco

RIO TEJO

0 _____ 400 m
0 _____ 0.2 miles

like *The Donkey and the Little Dog*. The tower offers captivating views over Alfama to the river.

○ MUSEU DE ARTES DECORATIVAS

Decorative Arts Museum; ☎ 218 814 651; www.fress.pt; Largo das Portas do Sol 2; adult/under 14yr/concession €4/free/2; ◷ 10am-5pm Tue-Sun; ▣ 28
Enter this petite 17th-century palace for a spin of decorative arts through the ages. Bedecked with original *azulejos,* chandeliers and frescoes, the lavish apartments creak under the weight of blingy French silverware, elaborate Indo-Chinese furniture and priceless Qing vases.

○ MUSEU DO FADO

Fado Museum; ☎ 218 823 470; www .museudofado.egeac.pt; Largo do Chafariz de Dentro 1; adult/concession €2.50/1.25; ◷ 10am-6pm Tue-Sun; Ⓜ Santa Apolónia

This engaging museum traces fado from its working-class Alfama roots to international fame. Alongside discs, recordings and posters, standouts include a recreated guitar workshop and hall of fame – look for fado queen Amália. Buy some fado of your own at the shop.

○ MUSEU DO TEATRO ROMANO

Roman Theatre Museum; ☎ 217 513 200; Pátio do Aljube 5; admission free; ◷ 10am-1pm & 2-6pm Tue-Sun; ▣ 28
This light-flooded museum opposite Sé catapults you back to Emperor Augustus' rule in Olissippo (Lisbon). The crowd-puller is the ruined Roman theatre, abandoned in the 4th century, buried in the 1755 earthquake and unearthed in 1964.

○ PANTEÃO NACIONAL

National Pantheon; ☎ 218 854 820; Campo de Santa Clara; adult/child €2/1, 10am-2pm Sun free; ◷ 10am-5pm Tue-Sun; ▣ 28

WORTH THE TRIP

Anyone interested in *azulejos* (tiles) won't glaze over at **Museu Nacional do Azulejo** (National Tile Museum; ☎ 218 100 340; Rua Madre de Deus 4; adult/concession €4/2, 10am-2pm Sun free; ◷ 2-6pm Tue, 10am-6pm Wed-Sun; ▣ 104, 105; ♿). Housed in a sublime 16th-century convent, the collection spans everything from early Moorish geometric tiles to Goan intricacies. The star exhibit is a 36m-long panel depicting pre-earthquake Lisbon. The cloister is a Manueline feast of weblike vaulting, twisted columns and blue-and-white *azulejos*. Upstairs, highlights feature a gold-smothered baroque chapel. Festooned with food-themed *azulejos*, the restaurant serves tasty snacks and opens onto a vine-clad courtyard. For more on *azulejos*, see p139.

Soaring above Graça, this sugar-white pantheon is a real baroque beauty. Its echoing dome is like a giant Fabergé egg – all pink marble and gold swirls. Note the cenotaphs to 15th-century explorer Vasco da Gama and *fadista* Amália before trudging up – phew, and up – 181 steps to the viewpoint, where Lisbon spreads out before you.

⊙ SÉ

Cathedral; ☎ 218 866 752; Largo da Sé; admission free; 🕙 9am-7pm; 🚊 28
Sé looks best when dusk light makes its bricks glow gold. The fortified Romanesque cathedral was built by Christians in 1150 on the ruins of a Moorish mosque. A rose window illuminates its cool, rib-vaulted interior. Note the impish gargoyles peeking above the orange trees on its southern flank.

🛍 SHOP

🛍 A ARTE DA TERRA
Gifts & Souvenirs
☎ 212 745 975; www.aartedaterra.pt; Rua Augusto Rosa 40; 🕙 11am-8pm Tue-Sat, 11am-6pm Sun; 🚊 28
Away in a manger of a centuries-old bishop's palace, this shop is worth a peek alone for its pebble floor and brick vaults. Bag authentic Portuguese crafts like embroidered love hankies and handpainted *azulejos*.

🛍 ARTICULA *Design*
☎ 934 113 225; http://teresamilheiro .com; Rua dos Remédios 102; 🕙 10am-5pm Mon, Tues,Thu & Fri, 10am-2pm Sat, closed Wed & Sun; 🚊 28
Rebel with a cause, Teresa Milheiro's anticonformist gallery-cum-workshop displays creations made from recycled bones, medical tubes and aluminium. Look out for doll's-eye necklace 'Big Brother is watching you' and syringe chain 'be botox, be beautiful'.

🛍 FEIRA DA LADRA *Market*
Thieves Market; Campo de Santa Clara; 🕙 7am-5pm Sat, 8am-noon Tue; 🚊 28
Get up with the lark to hunt for treasure among the tat at this lively flea market. It's all here:

Bag a bargain at the Feira da Ladra

granny's fur coat, back-of-a-truck sarongs, brass doorknobs, Neil Diamond LPs, droopy draws. Haggle hard and watch your wallet – it ain't called 'thieves market' for nothing.

GARRAFEIRA DA SÉ *Wine*
☎ 218 869 549; Rua de São João da Praça; ◷ 9am-7pm Mon-Sat; 🚊 28
Inebriating Lisboetas since 1927, this vaulted cellar behind Sé stocks 600 Portuguese wines and vintage ports. Try them first at the tasting tables.

PONTE LISBOA
Gifts & Souvenirs
☎ 912 421 929; Rua Augusto Rosa 21; ◷ 11am-5pm Mon-Wed, 11am-7pm Thu-Sat; 🚊 28
Blink and you'll miss this dinky shop with imaginative crafts by 15 Brazilian and Portuguese artists. Our favourites: Joana Areal's touchy-feely felt animals and Sebastião Lobo's glittering silver dragonflies.

🍴 EAT
BICA DO SAPATO *Fusion* €€€
☎ 218 810 320; Avenida Infante Dom Henrique; ◷ restaurant noon-2.30pm & 8-11.30pm Tue-Sat, dinner only Mon, sushi bar 7.30pm-1am Mon-Sat; Ⓜ Santa Apolónia
Actor John Malkovich has his fingers in lots of Lisbon pies, including this uberhip dockside venue

with space-pod lighting, crimson walls and floor-to-ceiling windows. Bica attracts a glam crowd keen to be sprinkled with Malkovich's celebrity stardust and nibble sushi or more ambitious highlights like suckling pig with Alentejo truffle.

BOTEQUIM SÃO MARTINHO
Tapas   €
☎ 218 860 215; Largo de São Martinho 1; ◷ 3pm-midnight; 🚊 28
Go retro at this tapas bar near Sé, plastered with Tricona sardine labels and quirkily lit by a dressmaker's model. Graze on chorizo and tangy cheeses with a glass of Alentejo white.

CASANOVA *Pizzeria*   €
☎ 218 877 532; Avenida Infante Dom Henrique; ◷ 12.30pm-1.30am Tue-Sun; 🚊 28
Perfectly thin and crisp, Casanova's wood-fired pizzas seduce the hungry lunchtime crowds. Snag a table on the riverfront terrace (heated in winter).

DIVINHA SEDUÇÃO
International   €€
☎ 218 888 144; Rua Augusto Rosa 4; ◷ 10am-9pm Tue-Thu, 10am-midnight Fri & Sat; 🚊 28
Gilt mirrors, fruit bowls that overflow and high-back chairs give Divinha Sedução a theatrical air. Locals praise its Med-style cuisine – think plump mussels,

shrimp cake with asparagus and passionfruit sorbet.

🍴 GRELHADOR DE ALFAMA
Portuguese €
☎ 218 886 298; Rua dos Remédios 135;
🕑 11am-2am Mon-Sat; 🚋 28

The decor is Flintstones meets fado at this cheery, no-fuss Alfama joint. Hear the sizzle, smell the barbecue and feast away on steak and fish grilled to perfection.

🍴 O FAZ FIGURA
Modern Portuguese €€€
☎ 218 868 901; Rua do Paraíso 15B;
🕑 12.30-3pm & 7.30-11pm, closed Mon lunch; Ⓜ Santa Apolónia

Cruise Alfama's backwaters to find this sleek, art-slung restaurant, rustling up innovative Portuguese fare. Dine in the conservatory for knockout views over Alfama and seasonal flavours such as wild boar with chestnuts or stingray in leek purée.

🍴 POIS CAFÉ *Cafe* €
☎ 218 862 497; Rua São João da Praça 93;
🕑 11am-8pm Tue-Sun; 🚋 28; Ⓥ 👶

Artists, bohos, mums with bubs…all have a soft spot for Pois. In capable Austrian hands, the cafe is terrific for lazing on a velvet sofa to drink coffee and crack the

Relaxed, fuss free and great food to boot – join the Lisboetas and stop to refuel at Pois Café

spine on a novel. The delicious salads and sarnies have Heidi-esque names – try Sepp (olive pesto, courgette and Emmental). There's a play area for tots.

🍴 PORTA D'ALFAMA
Portuguese   €
☎ 218 864 536; Rua de São João da Praça 17; ⏱ noon-3pm & 7.30-10pm; 🚋 28
Sardines hiss on the grill and owners break out into spontaneous song at this fado-crazed haunt. You'll find it hard to tear yourself away from the sunny terrace bang in Alfama's heart, especially with free *fado vadio* (amateur fado) at 3pm and 8pm on Saturdays.

🍴 RESTÔ *International*   €€
☎ 218 867 334; Costa do Castelo 7; ⏱ 7.30pm-2am Mon-Fri, noon-2am Sat & Sun; 🚋 28
Boho Restô is part of Chapitô arts cooperative. Sit in the leafy inner courtyard to munch tapas or juicy Argentine steaks. The upstairs restaurant has a safari stripe-and-spot decor; locals go really wild for the window tables offering mesmeric views to the river.

🍴 SANTO ANTONIO DE ALFAMA *Portuguese*   €€
☎ 218 881 328; Beco de São Miguel 7; ⏱ noon-6pm & 8pm-2am Wed-Mon; 🚋 28

Squashed between Alfama's houses, this bistro hides Lisbon's loveliest courtyard with vines, fluttering laundry and twittering budgies. Its vaulted interior is a silver-screen shrine, and the Vasconcelos brothers make a perfect double act, rolling out their own creations like Sophia Loren salad – an Italian pesto, rocket and salmon dream.

🍴 SENHORA MÃE
Modern Portuguese   €€
☎ 218 875 599; Largo de São Martinho 6-7; ⏱ 12.30pm-midnight Sun-Thu, 12.30pm-2am Fri & Sat Apr-Oct, dinner only Nov-Mar; 🚋 28
A drop of minimalist style in a touristy ocean, Senhora Mãe flaunts an almost-Scandinavian look with blond wood, clean lines and zinc flourishes. Dishes from venison in chestnut and *ginjinha* sauce to cuttlefish ink ravioli strike perfect pitch.

🍴 VIAGEM DE SABORES
International   €€
☎ 218 870 189; Rua São João da Praça 103; ⏱ 8-11pm Mon-Thu, 8pm-midnight Fri & Sat; 🚋 28; Ⓥ
Even Sé cathedral's gargoyles gaze longingly over to this culinary traveller. Your kindly host is João Baptista, the setting industrial cool with sci-fi quirks, like an illuminated zeppelin. On the menu: scallops flambéed in whiskey, slow-cooked Moroccan lamb,

chocolate cannelloni… Globetrotting here is moreish, we swear.

DRINK

▼ BAR DAS IMAGENS *Bar*

☎ 218 884 636; Calçada Marquês de Tancos 1; ⏰ 11am-2am Tue-Sat, 3-11pm Sun; 🚊 28

With the faintest ray of sunshine, locals flock to the postage-stamp terrace of this arty bar. Get giddy on Lisbon views and zesty *caipirinhas* as funky jazz plays.

▼ GINJA D'ALFAMA
Ginjinha Bar

Rua de São Pedro 12; ⏰ 9.30am-midnight Fri-Wed; 🚊 28

Tucked down a narrow alley, this hole-in-the-wall bar packs a cherry punch with *ginjinha* (€1 a pop). Natter with locals as those shots keep coming…

▼ ÚLTIMA SÉ *Bar*

☎ 218 860 053; Travessa do Almargem 1; ⏰ 6.30pm-1am Tue, Wed & Sun, 6.30pm-2am Thu-Sat; 🚊 28

Softly lit brick arches, bold contemporary art and DJs on the decks lure a young and lively crowd to Última Sé. Come for the sushi, expertly mixed cocktails and nights of world beats and reggae.

PLAY

Most fado places have a minimum charge of €15 to €25. Food is often mediocre, so it's worth asking if you can just order a bottle of wine. For the lowdown on fado, see p135.

★ A BAÎUCA *Fado*

☎ 218 867 284; Rua de São Miguel 20; minimum €25; ⏰ Thu-Mon; 🚊 28

Walking into A Baîuca is like gatecrashing a private family *festa* (party). During gutsy *fado vadio* performances, anyone can have a warble: feisty neighbours, gramps in the corner, the taxi driver… Spectators hiss if anyone pipes up during the singing.

★ CHAPITÔ *Theatre*

☎ 218 855 550; www.chapito.org; Costa do Castelo 1-7; ticket prices vary; ⏰ from 10pm; 🚊 28

Perched high above Lisbon, Chapitô stages alternative physical theatre performances. The jazz cafe downstairs hosts live music from Thursday to Saturday.

★ CLUBE DE FADO *Fado*

☎ 218 852 704; www.clube-de-fado .com; Rua de São João da Praça 94; minimum €10; ⏰ 9pm-2.30am Mon-Sat; 🚊 28

Vaulted and dimly lit, this is the place for professional fado, with a roll call of big-name *fadistas* such as Joana Amendoeira (see interview opposite), Miguel Capucho and celebrated guitarists like José Fontes Rocha. Arrive before the

Joana Amendoeira
Fadista and regular at Clube de Fado

What does fado mean to you? Fado is life itself: happiness, sadness, poetry, history. Every time I sing it's different, depending on the moment. I must *believe* what I sing, feel the lyrics with my heart. **And Alfama?** Alfama has a tight-knit fado community. We support each other like family. That's vital, as fado relies on harmonious, intuitive relationships between singers and musicians. **Any career highlights?** Performing with the brilliant guitarist José Fontes Rocha who composed for Amália. **What would you say are the best places for fado?** Clube de Fado for professional fado, Mesa de Frades for *fado vadio* – it's intimate and you might find a fado jam session there at 2am! **Future plans?** I'll be recording an album live at Castelo de São Jorge in 2008. But really I've already achieved my dream. I love fado, I love Lisbon. It's home.

show begins (around 10pm) to hear them hum and strum.

⭐ LUX *Club*
☎ 218 820 890; www.luxfragil.com; Avenida Infante Dom Henrique; cover €12; ⏰ 10pm-6am Tue-Sat; Ⓜ Santa Apolónia

Pulsating, eclectic, gorgeous – Lux is Lisbon's undisputed megaclub. With a razor-sharp design of mirrored tunnels and theatrical chandeliers, the dockside warehouse is the lovechild of Marcel Reis and John Malkovich. Top DJs like Leonaldo de Almeida and Pinkboy heat up dance floors with electro and house. Slip past the bouncers by 2am, as queues swell by 4am. Stay to see the sun rise over the Tejo from the roof terrace.

⭐ MESA DE FRADES *Fado*
☎ 917 029 436; Rua dos Remédios 139A; minimum €15; ⏰ 7pm-late Wed-Mon; 🚋 28

Small, local and bedecked with *azulejos,* Mesa de Frades is a magical place to hear authentic fado. Performances start around 10.30pm.

⭐ ONDA JAZZ *Live Music*
☎ 218 873 064; www.ondajazz.com; Arco de Jesus 7; admission €5-10; ⏰ 8pm-2am Tue-Thu, 8pm-3am Fri & Sat; 🚋 28

This vaulted, warmly lit cellar is the backbone of Alfama's jazz scene.

It draws serious music lovers with a stellar line-up of jazz, Latin and African gigs. Don't miss the free jam sessions on Wednesdays.

⭐ PARREIRINHA DE ALFAMA *Fado*
☎ 218 868 209; Beco do Espírito Santo 1; minimum €15; ⏰ 8pm-2am; 🚋 28

Top *fadistas* give their vocal cords a workout at this old-world haunt, owned by fado legend Argentina Santos. Performances begin around 9pm, but warm up later.

WALKING TOUR
ATMOSPHERIC ALFAMA

Have your camera ready as you're starting your walk on a high at **Miradouro da Senhora do Monte (1**; p65), affording sweeping views over Lisbon that reach from Castelo de São Jorge to Cristo Rei. Head south on Calçada do Monte, veering east along Rua Damasceno Monteiro, then down Rua da Graça to Largo da Graça, pausing to admire Villa Sousa's geometric *azulejos* as you cross the leafy square to **Miradouro da Graça (2**; p65). If the sun's out, kick back with a drink on the pine-shaded terrace for terrific vistas over Alfama's maze to the sparkling Rio Tejo.

Backtrack across the square and follow the cobbled Travessa das Mónicas onto Rua de São Vicente where the slender towers of 12th-century **Igreja de São Vicente da Fora** (**3**; p65) and tram 28 slide into view. Nip into the monastery to admire exquisite *azulejos* in the cloisters and panoramic views from the tower. When you're done, descend Arco Grande de Cima, with its stone arch and

snapshot river views, to Campo de Santa Clara. Bustling flea market **Feira da Ladra** (**4**; p69) draws eagle-eyed bargain hunters here on Wednesdays and Saturdays. On the opposite side of the square, the dazzling white dome of **Panteão Nacional** (**5**; p68) rises before

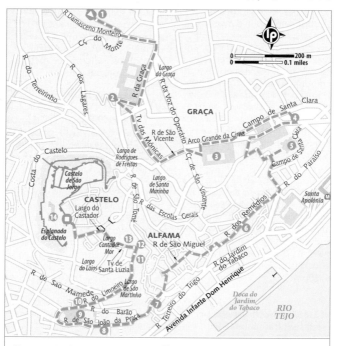

distance 3.5km **duration** Five to six hours ▶ **start** Miradouro da Senhora do Monte ● **end** Castelo de São Jorge

you; scale it for yet more dizzying views.

Walk down the hill to enter Alfama's web of steeply slanting lanes. Tread the cobbles along Rua dos Remédios, peppered with houses in sweet-shop shades that harbour cafes, grocers and galleries like **Articula** (**6**; p69). Now climb Calçadinha de Santo Estêvão onto Rua da Reguiera, veering left onto Rua de São Miguel. You'll soon reach Largo de São Miguel, one of Alfama's prettiest squares with its whitewashed chapel and lofty palm tree. Follow Rua de São Miguel onto Rua de São João da Praça, pausing on the sunny terrace of **Porta d'Alfama** (**7**; p72) for a sardine lunch, a pitcher of white and, if it's Saturday, excellent *fado vadio*.

Continue on Rua de São João da Praça and you'll pass some stunning *azulejos,* such as the diamond-point patterns at No 88 and floral motifs at No 106. Stop

for a caffeine fix at **Pois Café** (**8**; p71), then keep an eye out for the gargoyles as you approach the fortresslike, sand-hued **Sé** (**9**; p69). Just across the way, **Museu do Teatro Romano** (**10**; p68) traces Lisbon's Roman roots. It's soon time to grab the digicam again as you head up Rua do Limoeiro to capture knockout views over Alfama and Graça from the beautiful vine-draped **Miradouro de Santa Luzia** (**11**; p65) and Moorish gateway **Largo das Portas do Sol** (**12**; p65).

Cross over to the **Museu de Artes Decorativas** (**13**; p68) for a dose of sublime decorative arts, before taking the narrow cobbled steps up Travessa de Santa Luzia. Buskers often entertain crowds on tree-shaded Largo do Castador where, if you look closely, you'll spy a quirky urinal sign outside Palácio Belmonte. End your walk with sweeping views over Lisbon from the hilltop fortifications of Moorish **Castelo de São Jorge** (**14**; p65).

>BELÉM

At first Belém seems almost villagey with its cobbles and chalk-hued houses. Yet down by the Tejo, it's like stepping into a 3D pop-up book on the Age of Discovery: the mighty prow of Padrão dos Descobrimentos and the fortified Torre de Belém painfully brilliant in the sunshine.

You can almost picture Vasco da Gama setting sail from Lisbon in 1497 to discover a sea route to India; the salt-encrusted footstep he left on Calicut's shore kick-starting 500 years of colonial rule. Or Manuel I pouring his newfound wealth into the fantastical Mosteiro dos Jerónimos, saving just a pinch of cinnamon for those rich *pastéis de nata* (custard tarts) still served at the Antiga Confeitaria.

Whether wallowing in nautical adventures or eyeballing Warhol at Colecção Berardo, there's inspiration – old and new – wherever you look. And at dusk, when the pitter-patter of tourist feet fades and soft light paints the twirling Manueline turrets gold, Belém is finally yours alone for the exploring.

BELÉM

◉ SEE
Jardim do Ultramar........**1** D2
Mosteiro dos Jerónimos...**2** C2
Museu Colecção Berardo..**3** B3
Museu de Marinha **4** C2
Museu Nacional de
  Arqueologia **5** C2
Museu Nacional dos
  Coches **6** D2
Padrão dos
  Descobrimentos..........**7** C3
Torre de Belém............**8** A4

⬛ SHOP
Loja CCB..........................**9** C3
Margarida Pimentel .....(see 9)
Vista Alegre.................**10** C3

🍴 EAT
Antiga Confeitaria
  de Belém **11** D2
Cafetaria Quadrante.....**12** C3
Estrela de Belém **13** E2
Floresta.......................**14** D3
Pão Pão Queijo
  Queijo ....(see 15)

Rosa dos Mares............**15** D2
Ton Xin.........................**16** C3

🍸 DRINK
Belém Bar Café............**17** F3
Enoteca de Belém **18** D2

⭐ PLAY
Centro Cultural de
  Belém ....(see 3)
Estádio do Restelo........**19** C1

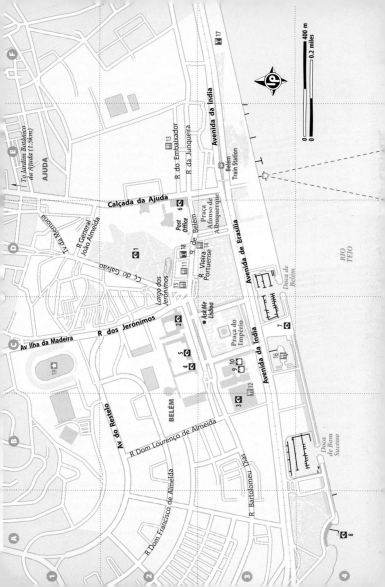

AJUDA

To Jardim Botânico
da Ajuda (1.5km)

R. do Embaixador

13

R. da Junqueira

Avenida da Índia

Belém
Train Station

Calçada da Ajuda

R. General
João Almeida

Tv. da Memória

Post
Office

6

R. de Belém

Praça
Afonso de
Albuquerque

Cç. do Galvão

1

18
11

15

R. Vieira
Portuense

14

Avenida de Brasília

Largo dos
Jerónimos

RIO
TEJO

Doca de
Belém

Av. Ilha da Madeira

R. dos Jerónimos

BELÉM

2

Ask Me
Lisboa

Praça do
Império

7

Av. do Restelo

5

4

9 10

16

3

12

Avenida da Índia

19

R Dom Lourenço de Almeida

R Dom Francisco de Almeida

R Bartolomeu Dias

Doca
de Bom
Sucesso

8

0   400 m
0   0.2 miles

17

◉ SEE

◉ JARDIM DO ULTRAMAR

Overseas Garden; Calçada do Galvão; adult/child €1.50/free; ⏲ **9am-7.30pm;** 🚊 **15,** 🚌 **27;** ♿ 🚼

This tropical garden cultivates 4000 species, from date palms to monkey puzzle trees. The bamboo-filled Macau garden is a botanical shrine to Portugal's former colony. Kids love to clamber over the banyan roots and spot the waddling ducks.

◉ MOSTEIRO DOS JERÓNIMOS

Hieronymites Monastery; ☎ **213 620 034; www.mosteirojeronimos.pt; Praça do Império; adult/under 14yr/concession €6/free/3, free 10am-2pm Sun;** ⏲ **10am-5pm Tue-Sun Oct-Apr, 10am-6pm May-Sep;** 🚊 **15,** 🚌 **27**

Belém's heart stealer is this bewitching monastery, built to trumpet Vasco da Gama's discovery of India in 1498. With its spindly turrets and filigree stonework, this Unesco World Heritage site is pure Manueline fantasy. For more, see p18.

◉ MUSEU COLECÇÃO BERARDO

Berardo Collection Museum; ☎ **213 612 400; Praça do Império; admission free;** ⏲ **10am-7pm, 10am-10pm Fri;** 🚊 **15,** 🚌 **27**

It's no secret that billionaire José Berardo's contemporary art stash

is among the world's best. What is news, however, is that this gallery presents his star-studded collection for free. A spin through abstract, surrealist and pop art reveals Warhol's blue-eyed girl *Judy Garland,* Lichtenstein's utterly dotty *Interior with Restful Painting* and Paula Rego's magical realism in *The Barn*. Picasso, Hockney and Pollock also form part of the picture. Niki de Saint Phalle's buxom *Swimmers* hog the limelight outside.

◉ MUSEU DE MARINHA

Naval Museum; ☎ **213 620 019; http://museu.marinha.pt; Praça do Império; adult/under 6yr/concession €3/free/1.50, free Sun 10am-1pm;** ⏲ **10am-5pm Tue-Sun Oct-Mar, 10am-6pm Apr-Sep;** 🚊 **15,** 🚌 **27;** ♿ 🚼

This nautical treasure trove flashes back to the Age of Discovery. Buried under model ships and cannonballs are gems like Vasco da Gama's portable wooden altar, the lavish private quarters of the 1900 UK-built royal yacht *Amélia* and magnificent galleons.

◉ MUSEU NACIONAL DE ARQUEOLOGIA

National Archaeology Museum; ☎ **213 620 000; Praça do Império; adult/under 14yr/concession €3/free/1.50, free 10am-1pm Sun;** ⏲ **10am-5pm Tue-Sun Oct-Mar, 10am-6pm Apr-Sep;** 🚊 **15,** 🚌 **27;** ♿

AHOY THERE, ERM, INDIA?

Vasco da Gama turned the tide on trade between Europe and Asia when his ship set sail from Lisbon in July 1497. After skirting the coast of Africa, the explorer washed up in Calicut, India, in May 1498 and received a frosty welcome from the Zamorin (Hindu ruler). His voyage was unquestionably heroic, but hardly plain sailing: monsoon tides were fraught with danger, scurvy was rife and more than half his party perished. For his pains, Manuel I made him a lord when he returned in 1499 and he was hailed 'Admiral of the Indian Ocean'. Luís Vaz de Camões recounts the adventures of Portugal's beloved *facundo capitão* (eloquent captain) in epic poem *The Lusiads* (p152).

Groaning under the weight of its riches, this museum spells out the past in artefacts – from Egyptian mummified crocodiles to Mesolithic flint stones. Particularly eerie is the Roman cult collection of phallic amulets and exorcism tables.

◉ MUSEU NACIONAL DOS COCHES

National Coach Museum; ☎ 213 610 850; www.museudoscoches-ipmuseus .pt; Praça Afonso de Albuquerque; adult/ concession €4/2, free 10am-2pm Sun; ☽ 10am-6pm Tue-Sun; ▣ 15, ▣ 27
Cinderella fans shall have a ball at this coach museum in the former royal riding stables. Its stuccoed, frescoed halls harbour one of the world's finest collections of coaches and saddlery. Jaw-droppers feature Pope Clement XI's scarlet-and-gold Coach of the Oceans.

◉ PADRÃO DOS DESCOBRIMENTOS

Discoveries Monument; ☎ 213 031 950; www.padraodosdescobrimentos.egeac.pt;

Avenida de Brasília; adult/under 12yr/ concession €2.50/free/1.50; ☽ 10am-6pm Tue-Sun Oct-Apr, 10am-7pm May-Sep; ▣ 15, ▣ 27
Like a mighty caravel about to set sail, this 52m-high monolith will have you reaching for the digicam. It was built in 1960 to mark the 500th anniversary of the death of Henry the Navigator (at the prow). Vasco da Gama and Fernão de Magalhães (Ferdinand Magellan) are among other explorers immortalised in stone. Whiz to the top for 360-degree vistas across the Tejo to Ponte 25 Abril. The mosaic in front of the monument charts the routes of Portuguese mariners.

◉ TORRE DE BELÉM

Belém Tower; ☎ 213 620 034; Avenida da Índia; adult/under 14yr/concession €4/free/2, free 10am-2pm Sun; ☽ 10am-5pm Tue-Sun Oct-Apr, 10am-6.30pm May-Sep; ▣ 15, ▣ 27
Nowhere is the lure of the Atlantic more powerful than at this

WORTH THE TRIP
Seek solace in **Jardim Botânico da Ajuda** (Ajuda Botanical Garden; ☎ 213 622 503; www.jardimbotanicodajuda.com; Calçada da Ajuda; adult/concession €2/1; ☼ 9am-6pm Oct-Mar, 9am-7pm Apr, 9am-8pm May-Sep; 🚋 18, 🚌 60; ♿ 👶) northeast of Belém. Dating to 1768, Lisbon's oldest botanical garden is ideal for a languid stroll with its gurgling fountains, manicured baroque parterres and mythical sculptures. Weave past lofty palms and bougainvillea, explore glasshouses nurturing ferns and orchids, or simply kick back on the lawns affording sublime views over Belém to the river.

Unesco-listed fortress jutting out onto the Tejo. Francisco de Arruda designed the pearly grey tower in 1515 to defend Lisbon's harbour. It's a Manueline treasure with delicate arches, meringuelike cupolas and plaited stonework. Venture down to the poky dungeons, before climbing to the top for striking views across the river. The stone rhinoceros below the western tower depicts the one Manuel I sent Pope Leo X in 1515, which inspired Dürer's famous woodcut.

🛍 SHOP
🛍 LOJA CCB *Design*
☎ 213 612 410; www.ccb.pt; Centro Cultural de Belém; ☼ 11am-8pm; 🚋 15, 🚌 27
There isn't a kitsch cockerel in sight at this forward-thinking design store, brimming with gadgets and knick-knacks from chic Eva Solo crockery to Mr P bathplugs.

🛍 MARGARIDA PIMENTEL *Fashion & Accessories*
☎ 213 660 034; Centro Cultural de Belém; ☼ 10am-9pm; 🚋 15, 🚌 27

Margarida Pimentel's ultrafine, nature-inspired jewellery fuses silver and gold with semiprecious stones. The designer's squiggly necklaces and bangles make snazzy gifts.

🛍 VISTA ALEGRE *Ceramics*
☎ 213 626 479; Centro Cultural de Belém; ☼ 10am-7pm; 🚋 15, 🚌 27
Porcelain lovers should check out Vista Alegre. Their exquisitely crafted dinnerware has been gracing Portugal's grandest tables – heads of state, royalty, you name it – since 1824.

EAT
🍽 ANTIGA CONFEITARIA DE BELÉM *Pastelaria*   €
☎ 213 637 423; www.pasteisdebelem .pt; Rua de Belém 84-92; ☼ 8am-midnight May-Oct, 8am-11pm Nov-Apr; 🚋 15, 🚌 27
A dieter's vision of hell, this patisserie has been transporting locals to sugar-coated nirvana since 1837. All hail the *pastéis de nata*, nests of crisp layers of pastry filled

Carlos Martins
Baker at Antiga Confeitaria de Belém

What's special about your job? Being part of a fantastic team. I've been here 30 years and still love baking unique *pastéis de Belém* and the whole hustle-bustle of the kitchen. **Is the secret recipe hard to keep?** Friends have begged for the recipe, but I'm sworn to secrecy and my lips are sealed. Even the 40 women that fold the *massa folhada* (puff pastry) into the baking tins don't see how the cream is made. The pastry cases are filled, then baked at 400°C to achieve that perfect brown crust. **And the competition?** There is no competition. You can only enjoy *pastéis de Belém* here, near Mosteiro dos Jerónimos where the recipe was invented. Our pastry is flakier and richer, our cream smoother. We turn out about 15,000 tarts a day, double at weekends. **Do you still eat *pastéis?*** Yes, only to control the quality, of course [smirks]

A tradition not to be missed – *pastéis de nata* (custard tarts) at the Antiga Confeitaria de Belém (p82)

with luscious cream and lightly dusted with cinnamon. The vaulted rooms pack in 2000 people, but part of the fun is devouring still-warm tarts at the counter. For more, see p19.

🍴 CAFETARIA QUADRANTE
Cafe €

☎ 213 622 722; Centro Cultural de Belém; 🕙 10am-8pm Mon-Fri, 10am-9pm Sat & Sun; 🚊 15, 🚌 27; Ⓥ

Get your art fix at Museu Colecçào Berardo (p80), then refuel over salads and soups at this light-filled cafe. Gallery-goers jostle for space on the terrace to admire Henry Moore's voluptuous reclining sculpture. Don't miss free jazz concerts at 10.30pm on Thursdays in summer.

🍴 ESTRELA DE BELÉM
Portuguese €

☎ 213 625 100; Rua do Embaixador 112; 🕙 noon-3pm & 7-10pm; 🚊 15, 🚌 27

In a sleepy backstreet, the star of Belém shines. Far from the madding crowd, this rustic place serves cold beer and soulful Portuguese grub, including herbed *salsichas* (sausages) from the local butcher.

🍴 FLORESTA *Portuguese* €

☎ 213 636 307; Praça Afonso de Albuquerque 1A; 🕙 noon-3pm & 7-10pm Tue-Sun; 🚊 15, 🚌 27

This down-to-earth bistro is a good lunchtime bet. When the sun's out, plant yourself on the terrace overlooking Belém's park. The grins of fellow diners munching fluffy omelettes and grilled sardines speak volumes.

🍴 PÃO PÃO QUEIJO QUEIJO
International   €

☎ 213 626 369; Rua de Belém 124;
🕐 8am-midnight Mon-Sat; 8am-8pm
Sun; 🚋 15, 🚌 27; Ⓥ

Savvy locals know the crisp felafel, sardine baguettes and spicy Mexican salads here are worth the wait. For a fistful of change, you can join them for several minutes of blissful chomping on the street.

🍴 ROSA DOS MARES
Portuguese   €€

☎ 213 637 277; Rua de Belém 110;
🕐 noon-3pm & 7-10pm Tue-Sun;
🚋 15, 🚌 27

Marshmallow-pink hues and country-cottage beams aside, Rosa is more stylish than twee. If it swims in the Atlantic, it's on the menu. Staff will help you navigate the seafood menu of lip-smacking morsels like shellfish rice and oven-baked *bacalhau* (cod).

🍴 TON XIN *International*   €€
☎ 213 016 652; Avenida de Brasília,
🕐 noon-1am; 🚋 15, 🚌 27

CELESTIAL SWEETS
The origins of heavenly *pastéis de Belém* stretch back to an early 19th-century sugarcane refinery next to Mosteiro dos Jerónimos. The liberal revolution swept through Portugal in 1820 and by 1834 all monasteries had been shut down, the monks expelled. Desperate to survive, some clerics saw the light in all that sugar and *pastéis de Belém* were born. The top-secret recipe hasn't changed since then and shall forever serve as a reminder that calories need not be sinful. Amen.

Flaming woks, a gut-busting €9.80 lunch buffet and a riverfront terrace lure folk to this Chinese den. Pile your plate with meat, fish and vegies, pick a sauce (*gon bao* adds a chilli kick) and let chefs work their stir-fry magic in the show kitchen.

🍸 DRINK
🍸 BELÉM BAR CAFÉ
Lounge Bar

☎ 213 624 232; www.belembarcafe
.com; Pavilhão Poente, Avenida de
Brasília; 🕐 10pm-2am Tue& Wed, midnight-5am Fri & Sat; 🚋 15, 🚌 27
Selfconsciously hip, the BBC draws fashionistas to its riverside lounge bar – all glass walls, violet lighting and leather sofas. The terrace is fab for savouring cocktails and views of twinkling Ponte 25 de Abril. DJ Espírito Santo heats up

the dance floor with hip hop and R 'n' B on Saturdays.

▼ ENOTECA DE BELÉM
Wine Bar

☎ 213 631 511; Travessa de Marta Pinto 10-12; ⏱ noon-10pm; 🚋 15, 🚌 27
Rated one of Lisbon's best *enotecas* by *Time Out Lisboa* in 2008, this tiny, friendly wine bar is a great introduction to Portuguese wine and port. Come to swirl, sniff and taste full-bodied Douro reds and lemony Alentejo whites.

⭐ PLAY

⭐ CENTRO CULTURAL DE BELÉM *Concert Hall*

☎ 213 612 400; www.ccb.pt; Praça do Império; tickets €5-40; 🚋 15, 🚌 27
Belém's cultural heavyweight, CCB stages first-rate performing arts. Its programme encompasses experimental jazz, contemporary ballet, boundary-crossing plays and performances by the Portuguese Chamber Orchestra. It hosts major events such as the Alkantara Festival (p24).

⭐ ESTÁDIO DO RESTELO
Stadium

☎ 213 010 461; www.osbelenenses .com; Avenida do Restelo; ticket prices vary; 🚋 15, 🚌 27
Catch a football match at this 32,500-seat stadium, built in 1956

and renovated in 2004. It's home to Lisbon's third team Os Belenenses. Views to the river from the west stand are superb. For more on football, see p140.

WALKING TOUR
CREAM OF BELÉM

Kick off your tour by immersing yourself in the crazed Manueline architecture of **Mosteiro dos Jerónimos** (**1**; p80) before the masses arrive. Nip into the adjacent **Museu Nacional de Arqueologia** (**2**; p80) to eyeball Egyptian mummies, or its neighbour **Museu de Marinha** (**3**; p80) for a romp through Portugal's seafaring past. Head back towards Largo dos Jerónimos, then swing a left onto Calçada do Galvão to seek respite under the date palms in the cool greenery of **Jardim do Ultramar** (**4**, p80). Backtrack to the old-world **Antiga Confeitaria de Belém** (**5**; p82), where a scrummy *pastel de nata* has your name on it. Now all that sugar and cinnamon has put a spring in your step, amble through the fountain-strewn gardens to the riverfront, where the shipshape **Padrão dos Descobrimentos** (**6**; p81) rises like a vision. Puff up 267 steps for far-reaching views or cheat by taking the lift. Cross back to Praça do Império, and head across the road for a brush with Picasso and Warhol at **Museu**

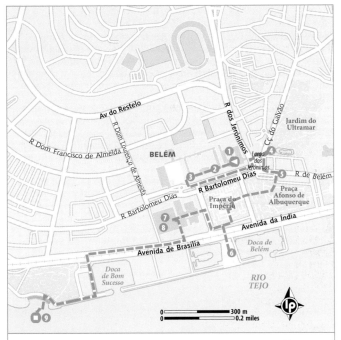

distance 3.5km **duration** Five to six hours ▶ **start** Mosteiro dos Jerónimos ● **end** Torre de Belém

Colecção Berardo (**7**; p80), part of the cavernous **Centro Cultural de Belém** (**8**; opposite). A brisk walk west along Avenida da Índia brings

you to the fortified **Torre de Belém** (**9**; p81), where you can still feel the intrepid spirit of the great Portuguese explorers of yore.

>PARQUE DAS NAÇÕES

Before Expo '98 few had heard of Parque das Nações (nas-*oish*), an industrial backwater northeast of Lisbon. Back then, the only sights were petroleum refineries, sewage treatment plants and slaughterhouses. The thou-shalt-clean-up-thy-act transformation happened almost overnight: filth-spewing smokestacks were demolished, slums bulldozed, locals rehoused. Magic.

What a difference a decade can make. Progressive architects, from Nick Jacobs to Santiago Calatrava, flexed their creative muscles and diligently revamped wasteland into a futuristic glass-and-steel playground, with an ocean theme and impeccable ecocredentials. By the time the world turned its attention to Lisbon, the polluting beast had become an ultra-modern beauty.

Today, families come to grin at the sharks in Europe's second-largest oceanarium, couples stride along the riverfront to the never-ending Ponte Vasco da Gama, and architecture buffs admire Gare do Oriente's vaulted splendour. Critics can say what they like about Parque das Nações being soulless; the truth is it spells out Lisbon's ability to successfully reinvent itself and embrace the future with gusto.

PARQUE DAS NAÇÕES

To Ponte
Vasco
da Gama
(900m)

Cursiva

R da Pimenta

Av de Boa Esperança

PARQUE
DAS
NAÇÕES

Rua do Bojador

19

Feira
Internacional
de Lisboa

3

12
17
11

OLIVAIS
NORTE

Rua do Bojador

2   Oriente

Gare do
Oriente

Posto de
Informação

1

20

22

15 Olivais

Lago das
Tágides

9

Homem-
Sol

Rossio dos
Mar Largo

Rhizome

18

14

Doca
dos
Olivais

10

13

RIO

TEJO

5

Cabo
Ruivo

6

4

21

Passeio de Neptuno

Alameda dos Oceanos

Av D João II

Av D João II

Passeio das Tágides

R D Fuas Roupinho

Av Infante Dom Henrique

0   600 m
0   0.4 mi

⊙ SEE

⊙ CAMINHO DA ÁGUA

Water Path; Alameda dos Oceanos; admission free; Ⓜ Oriente; ♿ ♿
Portuguese muralist Rigo designed this splash-happy boardwalk. Watch blue mosaic volcanoes erupt spontaneously or relax on one of the wave-shaped benches. Forget taking a dip, though, as signs warn that bathing is forbidden. Well, there's always the Tejo…

⊙ GARE DO ORIENTE

Oriente Station; Avenida D João II; Ⓜ Oriente; ♿
The brainchild of acclaimed Spanish architect Santiago Calatrava, Gare do Oriente is an extraordinary vaulted, vented structure. Its slender white columns fan out into a concertina roof to create the effect of a geometric, crystalline forest. The entrance, reminiscent of the *Starship Enterprise*, adds a sci-fi dimension to the colossal edifice. A trainspotter at heart, Calatrava has also pushed aesthetic boundaries at stations in Zurich, Lyon and Valencia.

⊙ JARDIM GARCIA DE ORTA

Garcia de Orta Garden; Rossio dos Olivais; admission free; Ⓜ Oriente; ♿ ♿
A botanical tribute to the Age of Discovery, this riverfront oasis bristles with exotic greenery. Keep your peepers open for rarities like Madeira's bird of paradise and serpentine dragon tree. A must-stroll is the Brazilian garden, shaded by bougainvillea, silk-cotton, frangipani and tabasco pepper trees. The garden is named after Garcia de Orta, a 16th-century Portuguese naturalist and pioneer of tropical medicine.

⊙ JARDINS D'ÁGUA

Water Gardens; Passeio de Neptuno; admission free; ☾ 24hr; Ⓜ Oriente; ♿

ART UNDERGROUND

Gare do Oriente became a showcase for Lisbon's boldest underground art at Expo '98 when it unveiled ocean-inspired sculptures and ceramic murals by internationally acclaimed artists. Be sure to glimpse Japanese Yayoi Kusama's cartoonlike creation resembling a space-age sea slug, Austrian rebel Friedensreich Hundertwasser's technicolour cityscape *Submersão Atlântida* (Submersion of Atlantis) and Argentine postmodernist Antonio Seguí's playful mural featuring butch-looking mermaids and a sinking *Titanic*. Equally intriguing is the dreamy seascape by Australian landscape painter Arthur Boyd and Icelandic pop artist Erro's mythology-infused work depicting buxom mermaids and writhing octopuses. For more details on *azulejos* (tiles) on the metro, see p139.

BARGAIN BOX

Save euros by purchasing the **Cartão do Parque** (adult/concession €17.50/9) for one-time admission to Parque das Nações' top attractions, including the Oceanário, Pavilhão do Conhecimento and Teleférico, plus other perks such as a 20% discount on bike rental. The pass is valid for one month, so there's no need to tick off the sights in a hurry. Bonus: the pass allows you to jump the queues at ticket offices. Buy yours at the **Posto de Informação** (Information Point; ☎ 218 919 333; www.parque dasnacoes.pt; Alameda dos Oceanos; 🕑 10am-8pm Apr-Oct, 10am-6pm Nov-Mar; Ⓜ Oriente).

These themed water gardens are a great spot to cool off in summer. When the sun shines, parents and their overexcited kids get soaked ducking behind the raging water-falls and misty geysers, and testing out the hands-on water activities.

⊙ OCEANÁRIO

Oceanarium; ☎ 218 917 002; www .oceanario.pt; Doca dos Olivais; adult/ under 3yr/under 12yr/family €11/ free/5.50/26.50; 🕑 10am-7pm Apr-Oct, 10am-6pm Nov-Mar; Ⓜ Oriente; 🚼 ♿
Surely even Nemo would sacrifice the reef for a swim in this mind-blowing oceanarium. Huge wrapa-round tanks give you the feeling of being underwater, as you come face to face with zebra sharks and

gliding mantas. The conservation-oriented oceanarium also arranges family activities from behind-the-scenes marine tours to sleeping – yeah right! – with the sharks. For the lowdown, see p17.

⊙ PAVILHÃO DO CONHECIMENTO

Knowledge Pavilion; ☎ 218 917 100; www.pavconhecimento.pt; Alameda dos Oceanos; adult/concession/family €7/3/15; 🕑 10am-6pm Tue-Fri, 11am-7pm Sat & Sun; Ⓜ Oriente; 🚼 ♿
Physics dull? Not at this temple to scientific wizardry, keeping little 'uns amused for hours with 'wowee' activities from launching

Kids have a ball at the Pavilhão do Conhecimento

hydrogen rockets to donning spacesuits for a walking-on-the-moon experience. Mini energy bundles run loose in the unfinished house – strictly no adults allowed! – while budding Einsteins have fun whipping up tornadoes, blowing massive soap bubbles and getting dizzy on the high-wire bicycle. Grown-ups secretly love this place too, Bill Clinton and Bill Gates included…

☉ PONTE VASCO DA GAMA
Vasco da Gama Bridge; Parque do Tejo;
Ⓜ **Oriente**
Dwarfing everything around it, Europe's longest bridge stretches a head-spinning 17.2km across the Tejo to vanish into the distance. Every detail was taken into account when erecting the six-lane, cable-style bridge for Expo '98, from the curvature of the earth to its rock-solid 85m foundations. Built to withstand a major earthquake and winds of up to 250km/h, it impresses with both its scale and statistics.

☉ TELEFÉRICO
Cable Car; ☎ **218 956 145; Passeio de Neptuno; adult/under 4yr/concession/ €3.90/free/2;** ⏰ **11am-7pm Mon-Fri, 10am-7pm Sat & Sun;** Ⓜ **Oriente**

The banks of the Rio Tejo provide an excellent vantage point from which to admire the Ponte Vasco da Gama

SCULPTURE VULTURE

Anyone interested in public art is in for a treat at Parque das Nações, where outdoor works created for Expo '98 feature star pieces by prolific sculptors such as Antony Gormley (of *Angel of the North* fame) and the late Jorge Vieira. The concept is that art should be tangible, with many sculptures designed to be touched, walked or climbed upon. Our favourites include:

> Antony Gormley's loose-limbed frenzy *Rhizome* on Rossio dos Olivais. The abstract iron sculpture represents nine life-sized human figures that harmoniously slot together.

> Jorge Vieira's iron-oxide *Homem-Sol* (Sun Man), a 20m anthropomorphic giant, whose sharp, angular bulk rises above Alameda dos Oceanos.

> Amy Yoes' totally loopy *Cursiva* near Torre Vasco da Gama, two lime-green iron squig-gles said to symbolise the capitulary of a medieval manuscript.

> Fernando Conduto's ocean-inspired *Mar Largo* on Rossio dos Olivais, a wavy mosaic pathway reflecting the tides of the Tejo.

> João Cutileiro's saucy *Lago das Tágides*, partially submerged marble sculptures of nude female figures that evoke poet Luís de Camões' mythical *Tágides* (nymphs of the Tejo).

Hitch a ride on this 20m-high cable car, linking Torre Vasco da Gama to the Oceanário. The ride affords bird's-eye views across Parque das Nações' skyline and the glittering Tejo that will have you burning up the pixels on your camera.

🔘 TORRE VASCO DA GAMA

Vasco da Gama Tower; Rua Cais das Naus; closed to the public; Ⓜ **Oriente**
You'd be forgiven for thinking you were in Dubai gazing up at this concrete-and-steel edifice, shaped like the sail of explorer Vasco da Gama's mighty caravel. Leonor Janeiro and Nick Jacobs were the architectural brains

behind the 145m-high skeleton, Portugal's tallest building. But the emaciated tower is about to be fed, with plans underway to convert it into a swish five-star hotel.

SHOP

🔲 CENTRO VASCO DA GAMA
Mall

☎ **218 930 600; www.centrovascoda gama.pt, in Portuguese; Avenida D João II;** 🕙 **10am-midnight Mon-Sat, 9am-1pm Sun;** Ⓜ **Oriente**
Water flows over the arched glass roof of this ultramodern mall, where young Lisboetas shop and hang out at the weekend.

The mall harbours high-street biggies like Zara, Diesel and Sephora, plus Portuguese names like Foreva, Vista Alegre and Continente. The multiscreen cinema and food court provide undercover entertainment on dreary days.

EAT

ART CAFÉ *Cafe* €
Alameda dos Oceanos; ☼ 8am-8pm Tue-Fri, noon-8pm Sat & Sun; Ⓜ Oriente; Ⓥ
Chilli-red walls glammed up with bold paintings give this high-ceilinged cafe an arty vibe. Relax over a *bica* (espresso) on the terrace or browse the menu for tasty salads, sandwiches and freshly squeezed juices. Free wi-fi.

ATANVÁ *Portuguese* €€
☎ 218 950 480; Rua da Pimenta 43-45; www.atanva.com; ☼ 12.30-3pm & 7.30-11pm; Ⓜ Oriente
The freshest Portuguese produce lands on your plate at riverfront Atanvá – think thin and juicy steaks, creamy Azeitão sheep's cheese and salt-crusted Atlantic sea bass. Grab a seat on the terrace to sip a glass of white and indulge in a little people-watching.

JOSHUA'S SHOARMA GRILL
International €
☎ 218 956 170; Rua da Pimenta 67-69; ☼ noon-1am Sun-Thu, noon-3am Fri & Sat; Ⓜ Oriente; Ⓥ
Shawarma fans head for this wallet-friendly snack bar for tasty kebabs, felafel and Greek salads. After dark it morphs into a relaxed bar, ideal for a beer and late-night munchies.

ORIGAMI SUSHI HOUSE
Sushi €€
☎ 218 967 132; www.origami-sushi house.com; Alameda dos Oceanos; ☼ 8-11pm Mon-Sat; Ⓜ Oriente
This light-flooded, Zen-style Japanese restaurant rolls out terrific sushi, sashimi and tempura. Its gallery-style interior is decked out with blond wood and cream stools. Forget fiddling with your napkin, instead try your hand at folding an animal to add to the origami zoo.

REAL INDIANA
International €€
☎ 218 960 303; Alameda dos Oceanos; www.realindiana.pt; ☼ noon-3pm & 7-11pm; Ⓜ Oriente
If you love Indian food, your tastebuds will do somersaults at Real Indiana. Far from your standard curry house, the decor here is stylish with brushed gold walls,

polished black tiles and eye-catching photographs of India. Well-executed offerings include fragrant biryanis, fiery vindaloos and perfectly crisp samosas.

REPÚBLICA DA CERVEJA
International €€

☎ 218 922 593; Passeio das Tágides; ☽ 12.30pm-1am; Ⓜ Oriente
Throw in a German chef and watch locals pour in for beer, carnivorous fare and a spritz of Teutonic tradition. This buzzy haunt churns out massive steaks in different guises – who's for oyster flavour? Daily specials are chalked on the blackboard. Weekend beer-guzzling sessions are complemented by ear-splitting live music and karaoke.

DRINK

Concentrated on the waterfront strip of Rua da Pimenta, Parque das Nações' nightlife scene is more slapstick than sophisticated. Still, there's plenty of choice when bars crank up after midnight. Check out the following places or let the groove lead you.

Ⓨ HAVANA *Bar*

☎ 218 957 116; Rua da Pimenta 115; ☽ noon-4am; Ⓜ Oriente, 🚌 208

The skinny-jean set rock up at this Cuban bar for hip-wiggling to Latin rhythms and *cuba libre* (rum, lime and cola) by the bucket. Skip the hit-and-miss menu and head straight for the dance floor. The glass walls offer superlative views of the Tejo and Ponte Vasco da Gama.

Ⓨ REAL REPÚBLICA DE COIMBRA *Bar*

☎ 218 956 056; Rua da Pimenta 65; ☽ 2pm-4am Tue-Sat; Ⓜ Oriente, 🚌 208

Students flock to this laid-back watering hole, recreating a Coimbra tavern with its stone floor, wooden benches and white tiles. Note the sketches and doodles of past punters dangling from the ceiling. It occasionally hosts gigs by up-and-coming Portuguese bands.

PLAY

☆ CASINO LISBOA *Casino*

☎ 218 929 000; www.casino-lisboa .pt; Alameda dos Oceanos; ☽ 3pm-3am Sun-Thu, 4pm-4am Fri & Sat; Ⓜ Oriente

The sibling rival of Estoril (p126), Lisbon's slick casino aims its chips at a younger crowd. Forget the James Bond–style tux, the dress code here is smart casual.

Ooh! Ah! Catch a show at Casino Lisboa (p95)

ON YER BIKE!

With its pedestrianised promenades and landmark-studded waterfront, Parque das Nações is custom-made for two-wheel adventures, particularly if you fancy freewheeling along the riverfront to the Ponte Vasco da Gama. **Tejo Bike** (☎ 218 919 333; www.tejobike.pt; Alameda dos Oceanos; per hr adult/child/go-kart €4/3/6; ☼ 10am-8pm Apr-Oct, 11am-6pm Nov-Mar; Ⓜ Oriente; ♿) rents out reliable sets of wheels including city bikes, kids' bikes and go-karts. It's located next to the Posto de Informação and Pavilhão Atlântico.

Aside from 1000 slot machines, 22 gaming tables and three restaurants, the casino hosts glitzy shows like *Stomp* in the revolving Arena Lounge. Branded a white elephant when it opened in 2006, the casino has played its cards right recently to boost its popularity.

⬛ FEIRA INTERNACIONAL DE LISBOA *Exhibition Venue*

Lisbon International Fair; ☎ 218 921 500; www.fil.pt; Rua do Bojador; tickets free-€8; Ⓜ Oriente; ♿
Designed by Portuguese architects Barreiros Ferreira and França

Dória, the striking, crystalline FIL is Lisbon's premier venue for exhibitions and trade fairs. Check the website for details of upcoming events such as Art Lisboa (p26) in November.

⬛ PAVILHÃO ATLÂNTICO *Concert Hall*

Atlantic Pavilion; ☎ 218 918 409; www .pavilhaoatlantico.pt; Rossio dos Olivais; tickets €15-40; Ⓜ Oriente; ♿
The spaceship has landed! Designed by dream duo Regino Cruz and SOM London, this UFO of sorts dazzles with an energy-efficient zinc roof. Portugal's largest indoor arena, it stages major international concerts, headlined by acts from

Madonna to Depeche Mode, plus other big events like freestyle bike and tennis championships.

⭐ **TEATRO CAMÕES** *Theatre*
Camões Theatre; ☎ 218 923 477; www .cnb.pt; Passeio de Neptuno; tickets €5-40; Ⓜ Oriente; ♿

Manuel Salgado's concrete-and-glass oblong, Teatro Camões is home to the Portuguese National Ballet Company under the direction of Vasco Wellenkamp. The choreographer has channelled his artistic vision into dance performances that thrill audiences with fluidity and emotional intensity.

>MARQUÊS DE POMBAL, RATO & SALDANHA

Any illusion about Lisbon being a cluster of villages is soon dispelled up north, where cute becomes cutting-edge: high-rises stud the skyline, traffic swirls around Marquês de Pombal and uptown girls go Gucci in designer boutiques. Perfect for a shop 'n' stroll is 19th-century boulevard Avenida da Liberdade, which poet Fernando Pessoa dubbed 'the finest artery in Lisbon'. Its 1.3km stretch of palms, cobbled mosaics and cafes links Restauradores to Praça Marquês de Pombal and timelines Lisbon from past to present.

A jump to the west, Rato reveals botanical verdure at Jardim Botânico and the loopy Aqueduto das Águas Livres. While a step to the north, bustling Saldanha reveals hotbeds in Parque Eduardo VII and high culture at Museu Calouste Gulbenkian, sheltering Rodin's eternal embrace and René Lalique's glitterbugs. Foodies book for top tables such as Olivier Avenida and Michelin-starred Eleven.

MARQUÊS DE POMBAL, RATO & SALDANHA

SEE

◉ CENTRO DE ARTE MODERNA

Modern Art Centre; ☎ 217 823 474; www.camjap.gulbenkian.pt; Rua Dr Nicolau de Bettencourt; adult/under 12yr/concession €4/free/2, free Sun; ◷ 10am-6pm Tue-Sun; Ⓜ São Sebastião

This avant-garde gallery houses a stellar collection of 20th-century Portuguese and international art, including David Hockney and Anthony Gormley works. Keep an eye out for Paula Rego's warped fairy-tale *Proies Wall* and Sonia Delaunay's geometrically bold *Chanteur Flamenco*. There's also a well-stocked bookshop and garden cafe. Revive art-weary eyes with an amble of the sculpture-dotted gardens.

◉ ESTUFAS

Greenhouses; Rua Castilho; adult/under 12yr €1.61/free; ◷ 9am-4.30pm Oct-Apr, 9am-5.30pm May-Sep; Ⓜ Parque

Tucked in a quiet pocket of Parque Eduardo VII (opposite), these 1910 glasshouses are perfect for a wander past greenery and tinkling waterfalls. The *estufa fría* (cool greenhouse) bristles with tree ferns and camellias, the steamy *estufa quente* (hot greenhouse) with coffee and mango trees, and the *estufa doce* (sweet greenhouse) with prickly cacti.

PIPE DREAMS

A spectacular feat of 18th-century engineering, Aqueduto das Águas Livres (Aqueduct of Free Waters) forces you to look up. Dom João V built it to bring Lisbon clean drinking water. Its 109 arches loop across the hills to Caneças, more than 18km away; they are most spectacular at Campolide, where the tallest arch rises a staggering 65m. On a gorier note, it's where mass murderer Diogo Alves robbed and pushed his victims over the edge, a crime for which he was sent to the gallows in 1841.

◉ JARDIM BOTÂNICO

Botanical Garden; ☎ 213 921 800; www.jb.ul.pt; Rua da Escola Politécnica 58; ◷ 9am-8pm Mon-Fri, 10am-8pm Sat & Sun Apr-Oct, 9am-6pm Nov-Mar; adult/under 6yr/concession €1.50/free/75¢; Ⓜ Avenida

Green-fingered students have lovingly nurtured this patch since 1873. The botanical star is the gigantic Moreton Bay fig near the entrance. Other species to look out for as you stroll include purple Madeiran geraniums, sequoias and fragrant jacarandas.

◉ MÃE D'ÁGUA

Mother of Water; ☎ 218 100 215; Praça das Amoreiras; admission €3; ◷ 10am-6pm Mon-Sat; Ⓜ Rato; ♿

The king laid the aqueduct's final stone at Lisbon's massive, 5500-cu-metre main reservoir.

Completed in 1834, the reservoir's cool, echoing chamber now hosts temporary art exhibitions. Be sure to explore the leafy Praça das Amoreiras, with its kiosk cafe, fountains and playground.

⊙ MUSEU CALOUSTE GULBENKIAN

☎ 217 823 461; www.museu.gulbenkian .pt; Avenida de Berna 45A; adult/under 12yr/concession €4/free/2, free Sun; ☺ 10am-6pm Tue-Sun; Ⓜ São Sebastião

Museu Calouste Gulbenkian shows an epic collection of Western and Eastern art. Your chronological romp begins with an antiquity feast of Egyptian mummy masks and Hellenic coins, intricate Persian carpets and grinning Qing Fo dogs. Stepping across to Europe, you'll gaze upon masterpieces of the Van Dyck and Rubens ilk. Highlights feature Rembrandt's *Portrait of an Old Man* and Rodin's passionate *Spring Kiss*. The climax is René Lalique's exquisite jewellery, including the otherworldly *Dragonfly*, glittering with gold, enamel, moonstones and diamonds. Don't miss free classical concerts at midday here on Sundays.

⊙ PARQUE EDUARDO VII

Alameda Edgar Cardoso; admission free; ☺ 24hr; Ⓜ Parque; ♿

If symmetrical box hedges and clipped lawns don't give away

Let *Flora* (1837) ponder you pondering great art of the East and West at the Museu Calouste Gulbenkian

this park's British roots, the name should. Edward VII visited Lisbon in 1903 and this urban haven is dedicated to his highness. The parterre affords sweeping views across Praça Marquês de Pombal to the azure Tejo. Retreat to its palm-shaded corners and lush *estufas* (p100).

SHOP

AMOREIRAS *Mall*
☎ 213 810 200; Avenida Duarte Pacheco; ☼ 10am-11pm; Ⓜ Rato
Amoreiras is a beast of a shopping mall with 275 stores, restaurants and a multiplex cinema. It shelters all high-street biggies including Mango, Swatch and Foreva.

ARQUITECTÓNICA *Design*
☎ 213 979 605; Rua da Escola Politécnica 94; ☼ 10.30am-7.30pm Mon-Sat; Ⓜ Rato

---

GUCCI, SWEETIE

Paris has the Champs-Élysées, London Regent Street and Lisbon Avenida da Liberdade. If you're after designer threads, this tree-flanked boulevard offers serious boutique satisfaction. Couture biggies to make your credit card splutter include Prada, Jimmy Choo, Armani, Louis Vuitton and Gucci. You could, of course, always indulge in the thriftier art of *ver vitrinas* (window shopping).

Straight from the pages of a lifestyle magazine, Arquitectónica is a temple to interior design, with everything from bubble-shaped lamps and sculpted log stools to vibrant crockery and rope jewellery.

CHARCUTARIA BRASIL *Gourmet Food*
☎ 213 885 644; Rua Alexandre Herculano 90; ☼ 8am-9pm Mon-Fri, 8am-2pm Sat; Ⓜ Rato
Planning a picnic in the park? Graze the shelves of this old-school deli for mouth-watering sausage, ham, cheese and port. The takeaway counter serves tasty spit-roast birds.

EL CORTE INGLÉS *Department Store*
☎ 213 711 700; Avenida António Augusto de Aguiar 31; ☼ 10am-10pm Mon-Thu, 10am-11.30pm Fri & Sat; Ⓜ São Sebastião
This Spanish giant offers nine levels of consumer heaven. Aside from the usual fashion, cosmetics and food court, it shelters cafes and a 14-screen cinema.

LIVRARIA BUCHHOLZ *Books*
☎ 213 170 580; Rua Duque de Palmela 4; ☼ 9am-7pm Mon-Fri, 9am-1pm Sat; Ⓜ Marquês de Pombal
Livraria Buchholz stocks one of Lisbon's meatiest collections of

English, French and German fiction, plus art books for those that *fala* (speak) a little Portuguese.

MONTES DE SABOR
Gourmet Food

☎ 213 962 337; Rua da São Mamede 103; ⏰ 10am-7pm Mon-Sat; 🚌 773
This is the go-to place for Alentejo specialities such as mountain honey, piri-piri sauce, olive oil and fig aguardiente. Planning a picnic? Stock up on *pata negra* (cured ham) and creamy goat's cheese from the fresh counter.

🍴 EAT
🍴 CASA DA COMIDA
Portuguese €€€

☎ 213 885 376; www.casadacomida.pt; Travessa das Amoreiras 1; ⏰ 1-3pm & 8-11pm Mon-Fri, 8-11pm Sat; Ⓜ Rato
With its ferny courtyard and antique-filled rooms, this sublime mansion is ideal for romantic tête-à-têtes. Delicacies like roast kid with herbs are served high and mighty on silver platters. The owners might even welcome you with a free glass of champagne; now *that's* service.

🍴 CERVEJARIA RIBADOURO
Portuguese €€

☎ 213 549 411; Rua do Salitre 2; ⏰ noon-3pm & 7.30pm-midnight; Ⓜ Avenida

See your dinner swim in the tank as you enter this beer hall, which locals hail for its fresh shellfish and buzzy vibe. Order a cold one at the bar because, unless you've booked, you're in for a wait.

🍴 ELEVEN
Modern Portuguese €€€

☎ 213 862 211; www.restaurant eleven.com; Rua Marquês da Fronteira; ⏰ 12.30-3pm & 7.30-11pm Mon-Sat; Ⓜ Marquês de Pombal
The merest whisper of Eleven makes foodies drool over the pages of their Michelin guide. With its killer location above

Getting ready for a foodie feast at Eleven

NEIGHBOURHOODS

MARQUÊS DE POMBAL, RATO & SALDANHA

Parque Eduardo VII, this Michelin-starred haunt is all glass walls, clean lines and Joana Vasconcelos art. Chef Joachim Koerper hits you with seasonal flavour bombs like sardine delight with artichoke and olive-oil ice cream, and black pork with cumin gnocchi.

🍴 LOTUS *International* €
☎ 966 970 421; Avenida Duque d'Ávila; 🕐 12-3pm, 7-10pm Mon-Sat; Ⓜ Saldanha; Ⓥ
Forget limp lettuce, this Bud-dhism-inspired newcomer rustles up tasty no-meat buffets for a wallet-pleasing €9.80. The sunny courtyard is ideal for sipping imaginative teas for lords, lovers and tigers.

🍴 LUCA *International* €€
☎ 213 150 212; www.luca.pt; Rua de Santa Marta 35A; 🕐 12.30-3pm & 8-11pm Mon-Thu, 12.30-3pm & 8pm-midnight Fri, 8pm-midnight Sat; Ⓜ Avenida
Lisbon's favourite Italian job, Luca runs like a well-oiled Vespa with creative Italian fare, snappy service and a slick interior festooned with black-and-white shots of pouting Hollywood divas. Staples like king prawn and lime ravioli go brilliantly with a bottle of Pinot Grigio.

🍴 OLIVIER AVENIDA
Modern Portuguese €€€
☎ 213 174 105; Rua Júlio César Machado 7; 🕐 7-10.30am, 12.30-3pm & 7pm-midnight; Ⓜ Avenida
Hooray! Just when we thought star chef Olivier da Costa had his hands full with two, he pulls another rabbit out of the bag. And what a beauty. This split-level restaurant is truly gor-geous – think champagne hues, teardrop chandeliers and pearl-kissed chairs. Sip cocktails at the horseshoe-shaped bar before savouring dishes like tender Kobe beef and sharp apple sorbet. Makes you wonder when those Michelin reviewers will arrive…

🍴 OS TIBETANOS
International €
☎ 213 142 038; Rua do Salitre 117; 🕐 noon-2pm & 7.30-9.30pm Mon-Fri; Ⓜ Avenida; Ⓥ
Vegetarians make the pilgrim-age to this Tibetan gem, part of a Buddhism school. Retreat to the courtyard to feast away on daily specials like quiche or curry, polished off with fresh juices and fragrant rose-petal ice cream.

🍴 PANORAMA RESTAURANT
Modern Portuguese €€€
☎ 213 120 000; Rua Latino Coe-lho 1; 🕐 12.30-3pm & 7.30-11.30pm; Ⓜ Picoas
Slung high above Lisbon's rooftops, the Sheraton's 25th-

Olivier Da Costa
Lisbon-born chef and restaurateur

What inspired you to become a chef? My father was a chef and I grew up in the kitchen, experimenting with flavours. I wasn't so great at school [smiles] so instead of getting my first job, I got my first restaurant – Olivier (p46) in Bairro Alto. **Describe your cuisine** Mediterranean-style food with lots of heart. My menus are ingredient inspired, unfussy, fresh and flavourful. **Any personal favourites?** In Bairro Alto, octopus carpaccio then osso bucco (veal shank) in port wine sauce. At Avenida, I'd recommend the Kobe beef with mango chutney and raspberry vinaigrette, followed by chocolate coulant. **What has been your career highlight so far?** Doing the catering for the MTV Music Awards held in Lisbon in 2005. **Future plans?** To ensure my restaurants run like Swiss clockwork. Avenida is the last, three is enough!

floor restaurant basks in the glow of celebrity chef Henrique Sá Pessoa, hailed Portugal's Jamie Oliver. Conjurer of flavours and textures, Henrique's creations juggle fresh seasonal ingredients, from appetizers such as tiger prawns in vanilla olive oil to mains like rack of veal with truffle polenta.

TAMARIND *International* €€
☎ 213 466 080; Rua da Glória 43-45; ☺ noon-3pm & 7pm-midnight Sun-Fri, dinner only Sat; Ⓜ Restauradores; Ⓥ
David Walia pours culinary prowess into Indian dishes inflected with chilli, ginger and fresh herbs. Based on Ayurvedic principles, his pink-and-blue restaurant is an oasis of calm. Mop up the juices of rich prawn kormas and lamb curries with fluffy naans.

VERSAILLES *Pastelaria* €
☎ 213 546 340; Avenida da República 15A; ☺ 7.30am-10pm; Ⓜ Saldanha
This swish 1930s *pastelaria* (pastry shop) is a marble, chandelier and icing-sugar stucco confection, where well-coifed ladies devour cream cakes, florentines and the latest gossip. The bowtied waiters are the spitting image of Muppet Show's Statler and Waldorf. Honest.

DRINK
CHAFARIZ DO VINHO *Wine Bar*
☎ 213 422 079; www.chafarizdovinho .com; Rua Mãe d'Água; ☺ 6pm-2am Tue-Sun; Ⓜ Avenida
In the centuries-old vaults of Lisbon's aqueduct, this beautiful *enoteca* (wine bar) pops the cork on wines handpicked by writer João Paulo Martins. Taste Portugal's finest, from Alentejo whites to Douro reds.

HOUSE OF VODKA *Bar*
☎ 213 259 880; Rua da Escola Politécnica 27; ☺ noon-3pm Mon-Fri, 7.30pm-late Mon-Sat; Ⓜ Avenida
This ice-blue bar inebriates locals with 300 different types of vodka. Purists go for Russian ones, while adventurous tipplers sample varieties like potato and fig. It also serves tasty Portuguese food laced with – you guessed it – vodka. *Nostrovia!*

LA CAFFÉ *Cafe*
☎ 213 256 736; Avenida da Liberdade 129; ☺ 9am-11pm Mon-Fri, 9am-midnight Sat; Ⓜ Avenida
With its art-slung walls and plump sofas, this laid-back cafe above Lanidor boutique is a great spot to rest shopping-weary feet. Free wi-fi.

Y LINHA D'ÁGUA *Cafe*
☎ 213 814 327; Jardim Amália Rodrigues; 🕙 10am-8pm; Ⓜ São Sebastião
When the sun's out, kick back on the lakefront terrace of this glass-walled cafe. It's an ideal coffee pit stop with greenery and a lively buzz.

⭐ PLAY

⭐ CABARET MAXIME
Live Music
☎ 213 467 090; www.cabaret-maxime
.com; Praça da Alegria 58; admission
€5-10; 🕙 10pm-4am Thu-Sat;
Ⓜ Avenida
In tribute to its former life as a Parisian-style cabaret, Maxime

has kept the scarlet walls and gilt mirrors, but bid farewell to the leggy showgirls. It now attracts young hipsters to its sweaty gigs of local bands, plus club nights where DJs play old-school tunes.

⭐ CAMPO PEQUENO
Bullfighting
☎ 217 932 442; www.campopequeno
.com; Avenida da República; admission €10-75; 🕙 10pm Thu Easter-Oct;
Ⓜ Campo Pequeno
Whether it ignites your passion or makes your blood boil, you can't ignore *tauromaquia* (bullfighting). Either way, the bullring itself is a stunner: a neo-Moorish

Betraying its bordello past – sensational and seductive surroundings at Cabaret Maxime bar

fantasy of red brick, bulbous domes and arabesque arches. For more on bullfighting, see p142.

⭐ CINEMATECA PORTUGUESA *Cinema*

☎ 213 596 200; www.cinemateca.pt; Rua Barata Salgueiro 39; 🕑 Mon-Sat; Ⓜ Avenida

The national film theatre screens home-grown and international art-house films in their original language, with occasional retrospectives honouring prolific film directors.

⭐ CULTURGEST *Theatre*

☎ 217 905 155; www.culturgest.pt; Rua do Arco do Cego; admission free-€18; Ⓜ Campo Pequeno

Experimental, nonconformist and often provocative, Culturgest's line-up spans contemporary exhibitions, dance, poetry, music and theatre.

⭐ FUNDAÇÃO CALOUSTE GULBENKIAN *Concert Hall*

☎ 217 935 131; www.musica.gulben kian.pt; Avenida de Berna; admission €10-30; Ⓜ Campo Pequeno

Fundação Calouste Gulbenkian delivers top-drawer musicians and first-rate acoustics. The roll-call has recently starred the revered likes of Russian pianist Boris Berezovsky. It's home to the Gulbenkian Orchestra under Lawrence Foster's baton.

⭐ HOT CLUBE DE PORTUGAL *Live Music*

☎ 213 467 369; www.hcp.pt; Praça da Alegria 39; 🕑 10pm-2am Tue-Sat, concerts at 11pm; Ⓜ Avenida

Dimly lit, nicotine-stained, poster-plastered Hot Clube has welcomed the cream of Lisbon's jazz crop since 1948. You'll have to shoehorn yourself into the cramped basement on a good night – it isn't called 'hot' for nothing.

DRIBBLING RIVALS

Football mad Lisbon is home to two of the country's three best teams: SL Benfica and Sporting Club de Portugal. They've been rivals ever since Sporting beat Benfica 2-1 in 1907. To catch a Benfica match, head northwest to the 65,000-seat **Estádio da Luz** (☎ 217 219 555; www .slbenfica.pt; Ⓜ Colégio Militar/Luz), where Euro 2004's big games were played and which supporters dub *a catedral* (the cathedral). Alternatively, see Sporting play at the ultramodern **Estádio José de Alvalade** (☎ 217 514 069; www.sporting.pt; Ⓜ Campo Grande). For the lowdown on matches and tickets, see p140.

★ SÃO JORGE *Cinema*
☎ 213 579 144; Avenida da Liberdade 175; Ⓜ Avenida

Ever since this grand cinema opened in 1950 with *The Red Shoes,* film aficionados have been flocking here for mainstream and independent films, particularly during funky flick fest Indie Lisboa (p24).

NEIGHBOURHOODS

MARQUÊS DE POMBAL, RATO & SALDANHA

>ESTRELA, LAPA & DOCA DE ALCÂNTARA

Quite a contrast to their wild-child neighbour Bairro Alto, Estrela and Lapa exude a gentrified vibe in streets dotted with vine-clad mansions, leafy squares and galleries. The well-heeled districts receive just a trickle of visitors despite obvious charms like neoclassical Basílica da Estrela and Dürer originals in Museu Nacional de Arte Antiga. Go west to tiptoe off the tourist trail poking around antique shops and exploring lanes that swoop down to the glittering Tejo.

The dockside duo Doca de Alcântara and Doca de Santo Amaro have been staging their own industrial revolution. Derelict warehouses have morphed into flash restaurants, cultural hotspots like Museu do Oriente, and ubercool lounges such as Estado Líquido where DJs spin as hipsters nibble sushi. Bye-bye grime, hello glamour. After dark when the rumbling Ponte 25 de Abril lights up, clubbing heavyweights Kremlin and Kapital thump to house and garage anthems.

ESTRELA, LAPA & DOCA DE ALCÂNTARA

◉ SEE
Assembleia da República	1	F1
Basílica da Estrela	2	E1
Casa de Amália Rodrigues	3	F1
Cemitério dos Ingleses	4	E1
Jardim da Estrela	5	E1
Museu da Marioneta	6	F2
Museu do Oriente	7	C3
Museu Nacional de Arte Antiga	8	E3
Ponte 25 de Abril	9	B4

🛍 SHOP
Yron	10	F1

🍴 EAT
A Travessa	(see 6)	
Alcântara Café	11	B3
Café Apolo XI	12	E3
Doca Peixe	13	B4
Espalha Brasas	14	B4
Estado Líquido	15	F3
Kais	16	E3
Montado	17	F2
O Chá da Lapa	18	E3

🍸 DRINK
Hawaii	19	B4
Op Art Café	20	B4
Taberna e Artes	21	F2

⭐ PLAY
Art	(see 24)	
Blues Café	22	C3
Buddha Bar	23	B4
Fundação Oriente	(see 7)	
Kapital	24	E3
Kremlin	25	E3
Paradise Garage	26	C3
The Loft	27	F3

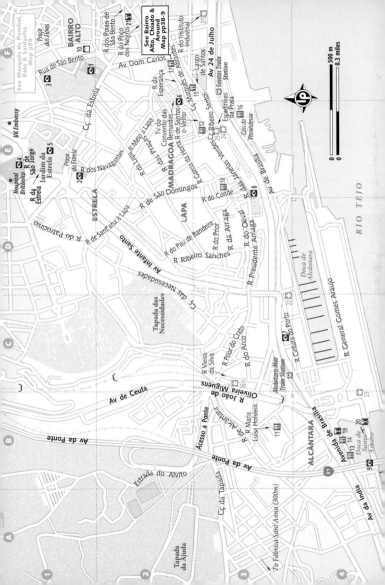

BAIRRO ALTO

See Marques de Pombal, Rato & Saldanha Map p99

Praça das Flores

R dos Poiais de São Bento 21
R do Poço dos Negros 21
See Bairro Alto, Chiado & Around Map pp38-9

10

3

R do Instituto Industrial

Rua de São Bento

Cç da Estrela

Av Dom Carlos

27

UK Embassy

R da Esperança
Av de Infantes
Largo de Santos
Santos Train Station
Av 24 de Julho

Hospital Britânico
4

R de São Jorge
Jardim da Estrela
5

R da Estrela
Praça da Estrela
2

R dos Navagantes

Tv do Convento das Bernardas
R de Santos-o-Velho
6
R Marquês de Abrantes
17
15
Cç Marquês de Abrantes
Escadinhas da Praia
16

MADRAGOA

ESTRELA

Cç da Estrela
R Garcia da Horta
R de Santos
R Vieira Portuense
12
25
R Ribeiro Santos
24
Cais do Sodré
Cais da Viscondessa

R de São Domingos
18
R das Laranjas
8
R do Conde

R de Sant'ana a Lapa

LAPA

Av de Brasília

R do Prior
R do Pau da Bandeira
R Ribeiro Sanches
R da Arriaga
R do Ouval
R Presidente Arriaga
R do Prior do Crato
R do Arco

Av das Necessidades

Tapada das Necessidades

Av de Ceuta

R Vieira da Silva
R Prior do Crato

R João de Oliveira Miguéns
Alcântara-Mar Train Station

R Cintura do Porto
22

Doca de Alcântara

RIO TEJO

Av de Ceuta

R Maria Luísa Holstein
11

Acesso à Ponte
Av da Ponte

R General Gomes Araújo

Estrada do Alvito

Cç da Tapada

To Fábrica Sant'Anna (300m)

Av da Índia

Av da Ponte

ALCÂNTARA

Doca de Santo Amaro
Avenida de Brasília
13 14
19
20
9
23

Tapada da Ajuda

0   500 m
0   0.3 miles

1   2   3   4
A   B   C   D   E   F

SEE

ASSEMBLEIA DA REPÚBLICA

Assembly of the Republic; Rua de São Bento; closed to the public; 🚌 49
All lofty arches, sculptures and Doric columns, the neoclassical Palácio de São Bento is the overblown yet still graceful home of Assembleia da República, Portugal's parliament.

BASÍLICA DA ESTRELA

☎ 213 960 915; Praça da Estrela; admission free; 🕑 8am-1pm & 3-8pm; 🚋 25, 28
The china-white dome of this basilica is visible from afar. It was completed in 1790 by order of Queen Maria I (whose tomb is here) in gratitude for a male heir. The echoing interior is striking come late afternoon when light streams through the candy-striped cupola.

CASA DE AMÁLIA RODRIGUES

☎ 213 971 896; Rua de São Bento 193; admission €5; 🕑 10am-1pm & 2-6pm Tue-Sun; 🚌 49
Fado fans make the pilgrimage to the former abode of superstar *fadista* Amália Rodrigues; note the graffiti on the street announcing it 'Rua Amália'. A 30-minute tour takes in glitzy costumes,

portraits and recordings of her performances.

CEMITÉRIO DOS INGLESES

English Cemetery; Rua de São Jorge; admission free; 🕑 daylight hours; 🚋 25, 28
Ring the bell to be buzzed into this enigmatic cemetery, overgrown with cypress trees. Expats at rest here include English novelist Henry Fielding (of *Tom Jones* fame), who visited Lisbon in vain in 1754 to boost his health and died two months later. For more, see p152.

JARDIM DA ESTRELA

Rua da Estrela; 🕑 7am-midnight; 🚋 25, 28; ♿
Escape the madding crowd at this oasis of greenery opposite the basilica. Kick back in the shade of a banyan tree, or wander twisting trails fringed with monkey puzzles, palms, willows and olives. Tots love the duck pond and animal-themed playground.

MUSEU DA MARIONETA

Puppet Museum; ☎ 213 942 810; Rua da Esperança 146; adult/concession €3/2; 🕑 10am-1pm & 2-6pm Tue-Sun; 🚌 706; ♿
This Geppetto's workshop of a museum enchants with rarities from delicate Burmese shadow and Chinese glove puppets to Javan rod creations and Sicilian opera marionettes. Keep an

eye out for Punch and Judy and their impish Russian sidekick Petruschka. Still think puppets are just for kids? Your nose is growing…

MUSEU DO ORIENTE

☎ 213 585 200; www.museudooriente .pt; Doca de Alcântara; adult/concession €4/2; 🕙 10am-6pm Wed-Mon, 10am-10pm Fri; 🚊 15, 🚌 18

The docks' biggest heart-stealer is this shrine to Asian culture, forging the link between Portugal and the East – from the first baby steps of the colonisers to ancestor worship. For the lowdown, see p21.

MUSEU NACIONAL DE ARTE ANTIGA

National Museum of Ancient Art; ☎ 213 912 800; www.mnarteantiga-ipmuseus .pt; Rua das Janelas Verdes 9; adult/concession €4/2, 10am-2pm Sun free; 🕙 2-6pm Tue, 10am-6pm Wed-Sun; 🚊 25

Set in a grand 17th-century palace, this museum presents a star-studded collection of European and Asian art. Must-sees feature Nuno Gonçalves' naturalistic *Panels of São Vicente,* Dürer's *St Jerome* and Courbet's bleak *Snow.* Other treasures include the gem-encrusted *Monstrance of Belém,* plus 16th-century Japanese screens

An effigy of *Yellamma* (Goddess of the Fallen) on display at the Museu do Oriente

depicting the arrival of the *namban* (southern barbarians), namely big-nosed Portuguese explorers.

PONTE 25 DE ABRIL
Doca de Santo Amaro; ⛴ 15, 🚌 28
If you experience déjà vu gazing up at this bombastic suspension bridge, it's because you *have* seen it before. The spitting image of San Francisco's Golden Gate Bridge, it was built by the same company in 1966 and is almost as long at 2.27km. It was Salazar Bridge until the 1974 revolution (p148) when a plucky demonstrator removed the 'Salazar' and daubed '25 de Abril' in its place.

SHOP
Fans of antiques and contemporary art should mosey down Rua de São Bento and Rua das Janelas Verdes.

FÁBRICA SANT'ANNA *Ceramics*
☎ 213 638 292; www.fabrica-santanna.com; Calçada da Boa-Hora 96; ⏰ 9am-12.30pm & 2-6pm Mon-Fri; 🚌 732
Azulejos (tiles) are synonymous with Lisbon. Fábrica Sant'Anna has been handmaking exquisite ceramics using traditional techniques since 1741. Take a spin of the showroom to discover the art and buy some of your own.

YRON *Design*
☎ 969 117 422, Rua de São Bento 170; ⏰ 2-8pm Mon-Sat; 🚌 706
Design junkies get their fix at this new gallery. Its temporary exhibitions showcase innovative work by home-grown creatives, with an accent on ecofriendly design. On our last visit: 21st-century Portuguese crafts including funky cockerels and cork stools.

EAT
A TRAVESSA *Portuguese* €€€
☎ 213 902 034; Travessa do Convento das Bernadas 12; ⏰ 12.30-3.30pm & 8pm-midnight Mon-Fri, dinner only Sat; ⛴ 25, 🚌 706
This 17th-century convent cranks up the romance with its serene

A DESIGN FOR LISBON
Lisbon-based architects, interior designers and artists have pooled their creativity into Santos Design District. The concept aims to promote forward-thinking design and give the district's galleries, bars, theatres and shops an injection of cool. Venues they've had a hand in and we've reviewed include Yron (right), Estado Líquido (p116), Museu Nacional de Arte Antiga (p113) and Montado (p117). For the nitty gritty, click onto www.santosdesigndistrict.com.

Alberto Bruno
Manager of Fábrica Sant'Anna

How are azulejos made at Fábrica Sant'Anna? Little has changed since 1741. Our 22 artisans still do everything by hand, from kneading and cutting to charcoal pouncing, glazing and painting. **Which are most popular?** Tricky. I'd say the classic blue-and-white geometric designs and culinary motifs for the kitchen. **And for Lisboetas?** *Azulejos* are so much a part of their daily life that often they're not really seen as art. **Why are your azulejos special?** They are handmade so no two are ever the same – a smidgen more ochre here, a millimetre extra there; some rough, some smooth. Each has its own charm. **What are the top places to see azulejos in Lisbon?** Palácio Nacional de Sintra (p22) for traditional *azulejos*, Lisbon metro stations (p139) for contemporary ones, especially stations like Campo Grande and Oriente.

cloisters and brick vaulting. António Moita whets appetites with fresh wood-fired bread and wild mushrooms in truffle oil, followed by delicacies like superb roast pork and walnut-prune semifreddo.

ALCÂNTARA CAFÉ
Modern Portuguese €€€

☎ 213 637 176; Rua Maria Luísa Holstein 15; ◷ 8pm-1am; ◻ 15, ◻ 28
Take the red velvet and polished wood of an art-deco brasserie, add innovative Portuguese cuisine, give it an industrial twist – eh voilà – you have Alcântara. This one-time warehouse offers Pigalle-style decor, an arm-long wine list and lip-smacking seafood with zingy sauces.

CAFÉ APOLO XI *Cafe* €

☎ 213 961 938; Rua de Santos-o-Velho 92; ◷ 6.30am-8pm Mon-Sat; ◻ 25, 74
Well-hidden from the camera-toting masses, this unassuming cafe attracts workaday crowds with daily specials such as tasty meatballs and stuffed cuttlefish.

DOCA PEIXE *Portuguese* €€€

☎ 213 973 565; Doca de Santo Amaro, Armazém 14; ◷ noon-3pm & 9.30pm-1am Tue-Sun; ◻ 15, ◻ 28
All hail this dockside restaurant for its incredibly fresh seafood; you'll see the main course in the

aquarium by the entrance. Virtually under thundering Ponte 25 de Abril, the terrace brims with Lisboetas devouring fishy specialities like lemony oysters or cod with clams.

ESPALHA BRASAS
International €€

☎ 213 962 059; Doca de Santo Amaro, Armazém 9; ◷ noon-1am Mon-Sat; ◻ 15, ◻ 28
A 1910 warehouse turned gallery-style restaurant, Espalha Brasas rustles up favourites like grilled chops and grouper with pine nuts. The dockside terrace is perfect for summertime chilling. Quirky touches: the nude sculpture and antique jukebox.

ESTADO LÍQUIDO *Sushi* €€

☎ 213 972 022; Largo de Santos 5A; ◷ 8pm-2am Sun-Wed, 8pm-3am Thu, 8pm-4am Fri & Sat; ◻ 15, ◻ 60
This ubercool lounge sports feng shui-inspired decor – think humbug-striped light panels, low seating and spacey lighting. Its mantra: unwind with a massage, then savour temaki sushi along with kiwi-fruit *caipirinhas*, before rolling your sumo belly downstairs where DJs pump electronica. Or head upstairs to the snowy white chillout room.

NEIGHBOURHOODS

ESTRELA, LAPA & DOCA DE ALCÂNTARA

🍴 KAIS *Fusion* €€€

☎ 213 932 930; Cais da Viscondessa;
🕐 8pm-midnight Mon-Thu, 8pm-1am
Fri & Sat; 🚋 15, 🚌 28

Cavernous brick warehouse turned foodie haunt, Kais exudes an industrial-chic air. Candles, jazz and sylvan touches like gnarled olive trees and cascading fountains soften the design. Signature dishes like duck carpaccio with black-olive pâté have locals whispering Michelin star.

🍴 MONTADO *Portuguese* €€

☎ 213 909 185; Calçada Marquês de Abrantes 40A; 🕐 7.30pm-midnight Tue-Thu, 7.30pm-1am Fri & Sat; 🚌 25, 74

Bemvindo carnivores! This cow-mad restaurant specialises in hand-reared organic beef from Alentejo's lush pastures. Feast on humungous steaks in vaulted surrounds, and keep an eye out for wacky touches like stag antler chandeliers and a bovine Mona Lisa.

Enjoy fast, fresh sushi in the funky lounge of Estado Liquido

🍴 O CHÁ DA LAPA *Cafe* €
☎ 213 900 888; Rua do Olival 6;
⏱ 9am-7pm; 🚌 60

Craving a cuppa? This ever-so-posh tearoom catapults you back to Victorian times with its flock wallpaper, gilt mirrors and matronly staff. Tea sipping locals can't get enough of its scones, dainty sandwiches and sticky éclairs.

🍸 DRINK
Hit Doca de Santo Amaro and Doca de Alcântara for waterfront tipples, a preclubbing vibe, and views of the glittering Ponte 25 de Abril.

🍸 HAWAII *Bar*
☎ 213 900 010; Doca de Santo Amaro;
⏱ 11pm-5am; 🚌 15, 🚌 28, 201

Young, flirty and fun in a rough-and-tumble kind of way, Hawaii attracts a youthful crowd of lads and bootylicious gals. Mojitos are cheap, Latino hip-wiggling plentiful and the surfboard straight from a Beach Boys' LP cover.

🍸 OP ART CAFÉ *Bar*
☎ 213 956 787; Doca de Santo Amaro;
⏱ 3pm-2am or 6am Tue-Sun; 🚌 15, 🚌 28, 201

Though just paces from other Docas joints, this glass-and-wood shoebox still feels like a well-kept secret. The waterside terrace is ideal for preclubbing bevvies. DJs spin house and lounge grooves till the sun rises at weekends.

🍸 TABERNA E ARTES *Bar*
☎ 960 268 035; Rua do Poço dos Negros 2; ⏱ 4pm-4am; 🚌 15, 🚌 28

Antônio runs this eccentric little bar and has filled it with vinyl (the placemats), dog-eared poetry books and Franco-era posters. Sip a cold one as flamenco plays.

⭐ PLAY
Bass-loaded, industrial-era Doca de Alcântara pulsates come *madrugada* (the small hours), as DJs heat up the dance floors in some of Lisbon's hottest clubs. Be prepared for the fashion police once-over.

⭐ ART *Lounge Bar/Club*
☎ 213 905 165; Avenida 24 de Julho 66; cover €5-10; ⏱ 9.30pm-4am; 🚌 15, 🚌 28, 201

A-list fashionistas and Moët-guzzling all-comers sway to house at this uberchic lounge before sashaying across to Kapital or Kremlin. The decor is as overdone as the ultrawhite smiles – think feather-filled columns and tear-drop chandeliers.

⭐ BLUES CAFÉ *Lounge Bar/Club*
☎ 213 957 085; Rua Cintura do Porto, Armazém 3; cover varies; ⏱ 8.30pm-

4am Tue-Thu, 8.30pm-5am Sat; 🚋 15, 🚌 28, 201

Kissed with gold and red velvet, this warehouse fuses 1920s glamour with industrial cool. Dark wood and tassel lamps add a nostalgic twist, while music skips from lounge to house. Chill on the dockside terrace. The party vibe picks up after 1am.

⭐ BUDDHA BAR
Lounge Bar/Club

☎ 213 950 555; www.buddha.com.pt; Gare Marítima de Alcântara 30; cover €10-20; 🕙 10pm-4am Tue-Thu, 10pm-6am Fri & Sat; 🚋 15, 🚌 28, 201

Mais ce n'est pas Paris! Never mind. Buddha still rocks with its chillout tunes, eye-candy crowd and slick oriental decor – picture exotic wood, Moroccan-style lamps and gold scatter cushions. The terrace has knockout river views.

⭐ FUNDAÇÃO ORIENTE
Concert Hall

☎ 213 585 244; www.foriente.pt; Doca de Alcântara; tickets €3-20; 🚋 15, 🚌 28, 201

Fundação Oriente's diverse line-up spans music, theatre, contemporary dance, puppetry and cinema. Expect everything from Tibetan overtone singing to art-house flicks.

⭐ KAPITAL *Club*

☎ 213 957 101; Avenida 24 de Julho 68; cover €10-20; 🕙 10.30pm-6am Tue-Sat; 10.30pm-4am Sun & Mon; 🚋 15, 🚌 28, 201

Make it past the goons at the door – being young, loaded and gorgeous helps – and you'll have a cracking night at Kapital. Ice-cool politicos and chichi Lisboetas defrost over hot garage and '80s tunes. The test: slipping into the VIP lounge (Paris Hilton's my cousin, honest…).

⭐ KREMLIN *Club*

☎ 213 525 867; Escadinhas da Praia 5; cover €10; 🕙 midnight-6am Tue-Thu, midnight-9am Fri & Sat; 🚋 15, 🚌 28, 201

Though this clubbing king's crown is lopsided since Lux (p75) stole the throne, it's still worthwhile if you get the nod from the Stalinesque doormen. Gays, straights and supermodel wannabes shuffle to deep house in oriental surrounds – elephants, Buddhas, the works. Heats up around 3am.

⭐ PARADISE GARAGE *Club*

☎ 217 904 080; Rua João de Oliveira Miguéns 38; cover varies; midnight-6am Thu-Sun; 🚌 60

Resident DJ Enrage and VJ Water keep the dance floor rammed playing mostly garage anthems. Saturday night's Baby Loves

Disco party and regular gigs draw an assorted bunch of gays and straights. Mercifully, it's not a beauty contest to get in.

⭐ THE LOFT *Club*
☎ 213 964 841; www.theloft.pt; Rua do Instituto Industrial 6; cover €5-15; 🕑 midnight-4am Wed-Thu, midnight-9.30am Fri & Sat; 🚊 15, 🚌 28, 201

Polkadotty walls, primary colour cube stools and violet lighting glam up this new kid on the dock. Grab a beanbag, order a *caipirinha* and join the Lisboan 20-some-things for house parties on the dance floor.

>DAY TRIPS

Take a lead from the locals – skip town to enjoy Praia do Tamariz at Estoril (p126)

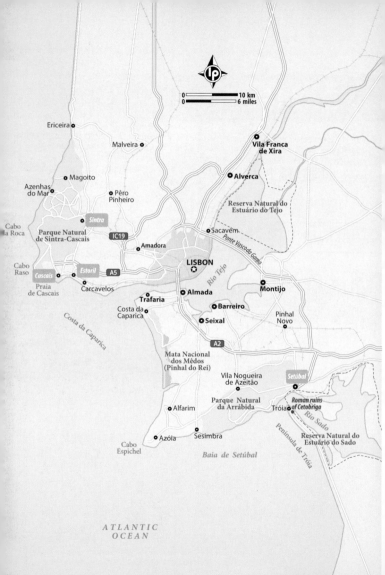

SETÚBAL

The thriving port of Setúbal (*shtoo*-bahl) is famous for lip-smacking sardines, but to admire its sublime natural assets, dip your toes into its watery backyard. **Parque Natural da Arrábida** is an ecocool beauty with scalloped Mediterranean-style bays, pine-brushed hills and vertical cliffs. Wildlife spotters make for the marshy **Reserva Natural do Estuário do Sado**, the splashy playground of 30 bottlenose dolphins, flocks of white storks, and 1000 wintering flamingos that make the water fizz like pink champagne.

But it's Flipper's frolicsome friends that hog the limelight. Boat trips to the Sado estuary almost guarantee sightings of the frisky, inquisitive fellas, who show off their dorsal fins to a happy-snappy audience. Listen for their high-pitched clicking as you cruise past. Dolphin-watching companies, charging €30-40 for a half-day tour, include **Vertigem Azul** (☎ 265 238 000; www.vertigemazul.com; Rua Praia da Saúde 11D) and **Mil Andanças** (☎ 265 532 996; www.mil-andancas.pt; Avenida Luísa Todi 121).

Back on dry land, saunter through Setúbal's pedestrianised centre, past Praça de Bocage's palms, arcades and dancing fountains to early-Manueline stunner **Igreja de Jesus** (Praça Miguel Bombarda; admission free; ⏱ 9am-1pm & 2-5.30pm Tue-Sun). Diogo de Boitaca let his fantasy run wild on this church in 1490, with its wispy turrets and twisting vinelike columns of pink Arrábida marble.

Setúbal's fish reeled in the Romans 2000 years ago. To see what all the fuss is about, head for the wall-to-wall seafood joints at the western end of Avenida Luísa Todi for hearty *caldeirada* (fish stew) or *choco frito* (fried cuttlefish) with sweet Muscat wine. A tasty pick with outdoor seating is **Casa Santiago** (☎ 265 221 688).

So long Setúbal, and thanks for all the fish.

INFORMATION

Location 47km southeast of Lisbon
Getting there 🚊 Terreiro do Paço to Barreiro (€1.75; 30 minutes; every 10 to 20 minutes), then 🚆 Barreiro to Setúbal (€1.70; 45 minutes; hourly); 🚗 Cross the Ponte 25 de Abril and head south on the A2 motorway (Autoestrada do Sul). The journey is 48km and takes approximately 45 minutes.
Contact www.mun-setubal.pt
When to go ⏱ Year-round

SINTRA

Sintra has a pinch-me quality with its rippling mountains, dewy forests thick with ferns, and fairy-tale palaces affording top-of-the-beanstalk views. Its Unesco World Heritage centre, **Sintra-Vila**, is a storybook of pastel-daubed villas folded into luxuriant hills that roll down to the blue Atlantic. And when Lisbon wilts in the heat, Sintra is a wet wipe with its cool microclimate. It's *the* must-do daytrip, but come midweek to avoid the crowds.

Celts worshipped their moon god here, the Moors built a precipitous fort and 18th-century Portuguese royals swanned around its dreamy gardens in summertime. Even Lord Byron waxed lyrical about Sintra's charms: 'Lo! Cintra's glorious Eden intervenes, in variegated maze of mount and glen', which inspired his epic poem *Childe Harold's Pilgrimage*. Extravagant and exquisite, Sintra has ivy-clad turrets for acting out Rapunzel fantasies, nature-gone-wild botanical gardens and forests strewn with megalithic granite boulders like ogres' marbles.

Sintra-Vila's heart-stealer is Bavarian-Manueline folly **Palácio Nacional de Sintra** (☎ 219 106 840; adult/under 15yr/concession €5/free/2, free 10am-2pm Sun; 🕑 10am-5.30pm Thu-Tue), whose iconic funnel-shaped chimneys grace every postcard. For more details, see p22. Nearby, **Quinta da Regaleira** (☎ 219 106 650; Rua Barbosa du Bocage; adult/under 14yr/concession €6/3/4; 🕑 10am-6.30pm Feb-Mar & Oct, 10am-8pm Apr-Sep, 10am-5.30pm Nov-Jan) is a frothy neo-Manueline villa set in fantastical gardens speckled with leering gargoyles, grottoes and lakes. Seek out the 30m initiation well, which spirals down to a warren of underground galleries lit by fairy lights.

A zigzagging, 50-minute hike through pine and eucalyptus woods brings you to the above-the-clouds **Palácio Nacional da Pena** (☎ 219 105

INFORMATION

Location 28km northwest of Lisbon
Getting there 🚆 Estação do Rossio to Sintra (€1.70; 40 minutes; every 20 to 30 minutes); 🚗 Head north of Lisbon on the IC19. The journey is 31km and takes around 35 minutes.
Contact www.cm-sintra.pt
When to go 🕑 Year-round

TOOTH FAIRIES

Sintra is known for its luscious sweeties. **Fábrica das Verdadeiras Queijadas da Sapa** (☎ 219 230 493; Volta do Duche 12) has been rotting the teeth of royalty since 1756 with bite-sized *queijadas*, crisp pastry shells filled with a marzipan-like mix of fresh cheese, sugar, flour and cinnamon. Since 1952, **Casa Piriquita** (☎ 219 230 626; Rua das Padarias 1-5) has been tempting locals with another sweet dream – the *travesseiro* (pillow), light puff pastry turned, rolled and folded seven times, then filled with delicious almond-and-egg-yolk cream and dusted with sugar.

340; www.parquesdesintra.pt; adult/under 5yr/concession €11/free/9, free 10am-2pm Sun; 9.45am-7.30pm Jun-Oct, 10am-6pm Nov-May). The wacky confection is a riot of onion domes, Moorish keyhole gates, writhing stone snakes, and crenellated towers in sherbet-bonbon pinks and lemons. It's the 1840 brainchild of Ferdinand of Saxe Coburg-Gotha, the husband of Queen Maria II and nephew – boy does it show! – of Bavaria's mad King Ludwig. Step inside to glimpse precious Meissen porcelain, Eiffel furniture, trompe l'oeil murals and Dom Carlos' unfinished nudes.

Soaring 412m above sea level, the mist-enshrouded **Castelo dos Mouros** (☎ 219 107 970; adult/concession €5/3; 9am-8pm May–mid-Sep, 10am-6pm mid-Sep–Apr) is a Great Wall of China in miniature. Like a dragon's backbone, this 9th-century Moorish castle's dizzying ramparts clamber and wriggle across the mountain ridges, past boulders the size of small buses. When the clouds peel away, the vistas over Sintra's palace-dotted hill and dale are – like the climb – breathtaking.

Back in Sintra-Vila, there's time to squeeze in a mooch around the cobbled **Escadinhas do Teixeira** and an art fix at the world-class **Museu de Arte Moderna** (☎ 219 248 170; Avenida Heliodoro Salgado; adult/under 18yr €3/free, 10am-2pm Sun free; 10am-6pm Tue-Sun), showcasing an outstanding postwar collection including works by Warhol, Lichtenstein, Pollock and Klein.

For pre-dinner *vinho* (wine) and nibbles, head to **Binhoteca** (☎ 219 240 849; Rua das Padarias 16) cellar, where you can sample full-bodied Douros and vintage ports by the glass and graze on local goodies such as cumin-and-apple blood sausage. **Tacho Real** (☎ 219 235 277; Rua da Ferraria 4) has a people-watching terrace on the cobbles and a 17th-century vaulted interior, where seafood fiends tuck into garlicky mussels and stuffed king crab.

CASCAIS & ESTORIL

Ever since King Luís I slipped his bathing togs on for a dip in 1870, Cascais (kush-*kaish*) has rocketed from sleepy fishing village to much-loved summertime playground of shiny, happy Lisboetas. Its trio of arching golden bays – Praia da Conceição, Praia da Rainha and Praia da Ribeira – attract sun-worshipping locals, families that come to splash in the icy-cold Atlantic, and boozing, schmoozing teenagers. It's good clean fun, but don't expect much sand to yourself at the weekend.

Eschew the flop-and-burn hordes in favour of a snoop around Cascais' cobbled heart. Sunny **Praça 5 de Outubro** charms with a Renaissance town hall festooned with cherubic *azulejos* (tiles) and wavelike mosaics that seem to wobble after a few Sagres beers. The lanes fanning out from the square brim with gelatarias, bars, alfresco bistros and chichi boutiques on Rua Frederico Arouca. Stick around for the buzzy **Fish Market** (✷ 5pm Mon-Sat), where grizzled auctioneers flog the day's catch in rapid-fire lingo.

Go west from Praia da Ribeira to saunter old-world alleys like Beco dos Invalides, filled with squat pastel houses, bougainvillea and birdsong. You'll emerge at tranquil **Parque Marechal Carmona** (Avenida da República; admission free; ✷ 8.30am-7.45pm), bristling with palms, pines and gnarled banyan trees. Kiddies love the ducks and playground, but the grimy mini-zoo is a letdown. Peeking above the foliage is canary-yellow **Museu Condes de Castro Guimarães** (☎ 214 825 407; admission €1.60; ✷ 10am-5pm Tue-Sun), Jorge O'Neill's mansion, where treasures include a tranquil cloister, oriental silks and a rare 16th-century manuscript of pre-earthquake Lisbon.

A mile-long coastal promenade, necklaced with sandy coves and strung with tiny fish restaurants, links Cascais to Estoril. Walk it or hire a bike for free at **Largo da Estação** (✷ 8am-7pm) by the train station. Once

INFORMATION

Location 29km west of Lisbon
Getting there 🚆 Cais do Sodré to Cascais via Estoril (€1.70; 40 minutes; every 20 to 30 minutes); 🚗 Follow the A5 west of Lisbon. The journey is 32km and takes approximately 35 minutes.
Contact www.visitestoril.com
When to go ✷ May-Sep

SURF'S UP

Pounded by massive rollers, Guincho, 7km northwest of Cascais, is a mecca to surfers, windsurfers and kiteboarders. Waves roll in from the cobalt Atlantic at this wild, dune-flanked beach, which has previously hosted World Surfing Championships. If you're keen to ride them, grab your boardies and check out the surfing courses available at **Moana Surf School** (☎ 964 449 436; www.moanasurfschool.com) and **Guincho Surf School** (☎ 965 059 421), or rent a board from **Aerial Wind e Surf** (☎ 917 890 036). The strong undertow can be perilous for swimmers, but Guincho still lures nonsurfers with its powder-soft sands, fresh seafood and magical sunsets.

hailed the Portuguese Riviera, nowadays Estoril is a shaken, not stirred mix of turreted 19th-century villas, palm-fringed lawns and beachside cafes. Overshadowed by chesspiece Chalet Barros, Praia de Tamariz draws young sunseekers to its free saltwater pool, but otherwise the sedate vibe is more Bournemouth than Monaco.

Estoril was a hotbed of spies and royal exiles in WWII. Bond fans after a spritz of espionage today head for glitzy **Casino Estoril** (☎ 214 667 700; www.casino -estoril.pt; Avenida Marginal; gaming room/slot machine room €4/free; ⏲ 3pm-3am), the inspiration for Ian Fleming's *Casino Royale*. Fritter away your euros on a high-stakes poker tournament or check out the spangly Las Vegas–style shows.

Back in Cascais, there are some terrific restaurants open year-round. **Jardim dos Frangos** (☎ 214 861 717; Avenida Marginal) serves sizzling chicken piripiri, Smartie-bright **Confraria** (☎ 214 834 614; Rua Luís Xavier Palmeirim 14) rustles up great sushi, while **A Carvoaria** (☎ 214 830 406; Rua João Luís de Moura 24) is a South African gem with hearty fare, from ostrich fillets to spicy *boerewors*, a traditional South African sausage dish. For ocean views and tasty seafood for next to nix, try **Esplanada Santa Marta** (☎ 960 118 616; Praia de Santa Marta).

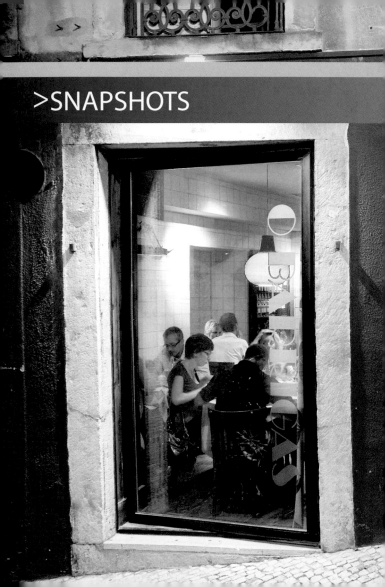

Whether you're a vintage diva or all-night clubber, design-conscious diner or botanical lover, there's a Lisbon to suit you. Find real fado, feel the pride in Príncipe Real, or seek out Rembrandts, Manueline architecture and cutting-edge *azulejos* (tiles). Sexy and nostalgic, cultured and effortlessly cool, Lisbon is a many-splendoured city.

Don't give it another thought – head inside to sample the treats at O Barrigas restaurant (p46)

SNAPSHOTS

ACCOMMODATION

Lisbon's hotel scene is finally waking up to those tourist euros. You can snooze in 18th-century palaces with castle views or bed-down in retro-hip digs in Baixa, crash in old-school guesthouses or join the A-list in monochrome designer pads with all the spa-and-cocktail-lounge trimmings.

Hot cookies are all-new design hotels such as born-again 1908 factory **Fontana Park** (www.fontanaparkhotel.com). Ultrasleek contenders include Belém's **Jerónimos 8** (www.jeronimos8.com) with a crisp aesthetic and art a-plenty. A central slicker is **Bairro Alto Hotel** (www.bairroaltohotel.com), revealing a razor-sharp eye for detail in its individually designed rooms.

Euro-economisers needn't get their pyjamas in a twist either, as hostels in Bairro Alto and Baixa have morphed from hospital-ward spartan to sublime. Many occupy revamped 19th-century townhouses with original quirks from stuccoed ceilings to *azulejos*. Their savvy owners offer perks from free wi-fi to communal kitchens and funky lounges. Sleeping beauties include the poetry-themed **Lisbon Poets Hostel** (www.lisbonpoetshostel.com), glam mansion **Oasis Lisboa** (www.oasislisboa.com) in indie-cool Santa Catarina, and the totally chilled **Goodnight Hostel** (http://goodnighthostel.com). All are supremely located for Bairro Alto's hedonistic nightlife and Baixa's high-street shopping.

Rossio and Bairro Alto favourites include cheery, atmospheric **Pensão Duque** (duquelisboa@yahoo.com) and art-nouveau charmer **Pensão Londres** (www.pensaolondres.com.pt). The sleepy, winding lanes of Alfama and Castelo hide sweet-and-petite guesthouses and palatial hotels with castle and river vistas. For the royal treatment check into restored 15th-century palace **Palácio Belmonte** (www.palaciobelmonte.com) near Castelo de São Jorge.

 Hotels & Hostels

Need a place to stay? Find and book it at lonelyplanet.com. Over 40 properties are featured for Lisbon – each personally visited, thoroughly reviewed and happily recommended by a Lonely Planet author. From hostels to high-end hotels, we've hunted out the places that will bring you unique and special experiences. Read independent reviews by authors and other travellers, and get practical information including amenities, maps and photos. Then reserve your room simply and securely via Hotels & Hostels – our online booking service. It's all at lonelyplanet.com/hotels.

Serene and leafy Lapa ups the romance stakes with boutique hotels in converted convents and palaces. Among the best are former nunnery with a modern twist **York House** (www.yorkhouselisboa.com), one-time 18th-century palace **As Janelas Verdes** (www.heritage.pt) and the dreamy **Lapa Palace** (www.lapapalace.com) set in mature gardens.

Another pocket of style is the area around Avenida da Liberdade and Praça da Figueira. Within staggering distance of boutiques and foodie haunts lie Cassiano Branco's modernist gem **Hotel Britânia** (www.heritage.pt) and aparthotel **VIP Eden** (www.viphotels.com), with its stunning rooftop pool.

Book ahead from June to mid-September when Lisbon's beds fill up fast. You'll pay roughly €20 for a dorm bed, €40 for a bare-bones double with shared bathroom and €80 for *pensões* with TV, air-con and breakfast. Hotel doubles start at around €80, with the plushest places charging up to €400. Expect discounts in the low season and for stays of more than a week. For self-catering apartments, costing €50-150 per night, click onto www .lisbon-apartments.com, www.lisbon-holiday-apartments.com or www .waytostay.com.

BEST HOSTELS
> Goodnight Hostel (http://goodnight hostel.com)
> Traveller's House Hostel (www.hostels central.com)
> Oasis Lisboa (www.oasislisboa.com)
> Lisbon Poets Hostel (www.lisbonpoets hostel.com)
> Lisbon Calling (lxcalling@gmail.com)

BEST BOUTIQUE HOTELS
> Lapa Palace (www.lapapalace.com)
> Solar dos Mouros (www.solardos mouros.pt)
> York House (www.yorkhouselisboa .com)
> Palácio Belmonte (www.palaciobel monte.com)
> As Janelas Verdes (www.heritage.pt)

BEST DESIGN PADS
> Jeronimos 8 (www.jeronimos8.com)
> Fontana Park (www.fontanapark hotel.com)
> Bairro Alto Hotel (www.bairroalto hotel.com)
> Hotel Britânia (www.heritage.pt)
> Anjo Azul (www.anjoazul.com)

BEST OLD-SCHOOL DIGS
> Pensão Duque (duquelisboa@yahoo .com)
> Pensão Londres (www.pensaolondres .com.pt)
> Casa de São Mamede (www.casa desaomamede.com)
> Sé Guesthouse (Rua São João da Praça 97)

SHOPPING

Lisbon is a fickle shopper: she's the glitzy, platform-shoed diva living vintage dreams in Bairro Alto, the couture lover prowling Avenida da Liberdade, the retro kid tied to granny's apron strings in Baixa and Rossio, and the high-street aficionado in Rato and Saldanha. Each of her neighbourhoods hooks shoppers with a different vibe and style.

Crackling with fresh-faced creatives and arbiters of vintage chic, Bairro Alto harbours Lisbon's coolest boutiques. Happy Days (p42) jives into the '50s with tutti-frutti prom dresses, El Dorado (p41) swirls with '60s psychedelic prints, while Agência 117 (p41) revamps your look with jelly-bean-bright dresses and glam locks. If rhinestone-studded flares are not your style, slip into slinky designer wear at Lena Aires (p42) and Fátima Lopes (p42), or track down Adidas one-offs at Sneakers Delight (p44). Emerging designers show their work at virginal-white Fabrico Infinito (p42), from recycled chandeliers to Jorge Moita's ultrafunky, jail-made La.Ga bags.

Well-heeled Chiado serves a mix of high-street and homegrown designer garb around Rua do Carmo (Map pp38–9) in beautifully restored

18th- and 19th-century buildings. Pick up sassy, feminine styles at the flagship Ana Salazar (p42), handmade gloves at wood-panelled Luvaria Ulisses (p42) and fairy-tale threads at Story Tailors (p44). For wacky souvenirs, check out the ever-so Wrong Shop (p44).

Baixa, Rossio and Alfama are Lisbon's Peter Pan generation, with old-fashioned service in timeless stores from haberdasheries on Rua da Conceição (p57) to retro-wrapped tinned sardines at Conserveira de Lisboa (p55) and hats for Bogart and Hepburn wannabes at Azevedo Rua (p55). Foodies head for Silva & Feijó (p57) for pungent cheeses and *pata negra* (cured ham), and Napoleão (p56) for top-notch Portuguese wine and port. For classic kitsch from cockerels to pocket-sized trams, explore Rua Augusta (p57).

Fashionistas splurge on ready-to-wear Gucci and Prada in the chichi boutiques lining boulevard Avenida da Liberdade (p102), or spend in Spanish retail giant El Corte Inglés (p102) slightly north.

Shops generally open from 9.30am to 7pm Monday to Friday and to midday Saturday. Bairro Alto is a late riser, with boutiques opening from 2pm to 10pm or midnight. Sunday? Forget it. Savvy shoppers hit the stores during post-Christmas winter sales and summer sales in July and August for savings of up to 70%.

BEST VINTAGE
> Agência 117 (p41)
> A Outra Face da Lua (p55)
> El Dorado (p41)
> Feira da Ladra (p69)
> Happy Days (p42)

BEST DESIGN
> Articula (p69)
> Fabrico Infinito (p42)
> Loja CCB (p82)
> Margarida Pimentel (p82)
> Yron (p114)

BEST SPECIALIST STORES
> A Carioca (p41)
> Azevedo Rua (p55)
> Conserveira de Lisboa (p55)
> Luvaria Ulisses (p42)
> Napoleão (p56)

BEST FASHION
> Ana Salazar (p42)
> Fátima Lopes (p42)
> Story Tailors (p44)
> The Loser Project (p44)
> Zed's Dad (p44)

Top left Unearth some vintage delights at Agência 117

FOOD

Once upon a time, chicken piri-piri was as spicy as it got in Lisbon's kitchens. Welcome to the happy ever after. Full of sparky designers, creative chefs and first-rate produce, the capital is extending its tentacles to new gastro waters. Grilled sardines on Alfama's cobbles and *pastéis de nata* (custard tarts) in old-school cafes still taste great, but save room for new temptations in celebrity haunts and Zen-style sushi lounges.

Alfresco diners are in their element in Bairro Alto, Alfama and Baixa. Ask to see the *menu do dia* for inexpensive daily specials. All-Portuguese favourites include vaulted beer hall Cervejaria Trindade (p45) for frothing beer and lobster stew, O Barrigas (p46) for lighter Mediterranean-style interpretations and too-sexy Pap'Açorda (p46) for namesake *açorda* (bread-and-shellfish stew).

Bairro Alto, Chiado and Doca de Alcântara dish up everything from authentic baltis to antipasti. Tamarind (p106) excites palates with Indian spice and ubercool Nood (p46) with stir-fried Japanese nosh. Your tastebuds will tango over Argentine steaks at Café Buenos Aires (p58) and Moroccan lamb at arty Viagem de Sabores (p72). At dockside Estado Líquido (p116), hipsters nibble sushi and get their feet rubbed as DJs spin house.

A new wave of star chefs are upping the antics at the stove with playful textures and seasonal flavours. Heaven's kitchens include Olivier Avenida (p104), the Sheraton's sky-high Panorama Restaurant (p104) and Michelin-starred Eleven (p103). For space-age design and innovative cuisine, book a table at John Malkovich's riverside Bica do Sapato (p70).

BEST ETHNIC
> Café Buenos Aires (p58)
> Luca (p104)
> Nood (p46)
> Tamarind (p106)
> Viagem de Sabores (p72)

BEST PORTUGUESE
> Cervejaria Trindade (p45)
> O Barrigas (p46)
> O Faz Figura (p71)
> Pap'Açorda (p46)
> Tavares Rico (p47)

FADO

Ask 10 Lisboetas to explain fado and you'll get 10 different versions. As one local put it: 'Fado is inexplicable, it's everything. It's life through the cry of a voice that's often also happy.' Moorish song and 16th-century ditties of homesick sailors have percolated the genre, and the blend can be as dark and powerful as espresso or as light and sweet as latté. *Saudade*, roughly 'longing', infiltrates all fado, while other themes are love, destiny, bullfighting and remorse.

Melodramatic and highly addictive, fado is a musical soap opera with its roots in the labyrinthine alleys of working-class Alfama. But fado queen Amália Rodrigues (1920–1999) made it famous with her heart-breaking trills and poetic soul. Revisit the early days listening to crackly recordings at Museu do Fado (p68) and Casa de Amália Rodrigues (p112).

Today, new generation *fadistas* are redefining the genre and broadening its scope; keeping the essence but giving it a bluesy twist, a pinch of Cuban *son* or a splash of Argentine tango. Big names to look out for include Cristina Branco, Joana Amendoeira (p74), Ana Moura and Latin Grammy-nominated Mariza. Discoteca Amália (p56) will bolster your collection.

Wandering Alfama by night, you'll hear the strains of mournful fado. Professional *fadistas* perform in the vaults of Clube de Fado (p73) and Parreirinha de Alfama (p75), but equally captivating are spontaneous *fado vadio* (amateur fado) performances that erupt anytime, anywhere; try A Baîuca (p73) and Mesa de Frades (p75). Quality varies from nightingale to turkey warbler, but performances are always heartfelt and fun.

BEST FADO PLAYLIST
> *The Art of Amália* (1998), Amália Rodrigues
> *Fado Em Mim* (2002) Mariza
> *Á Flor da Pele* (2006) Joana Amendoeira
> *Existir* (1990) Madredeus
> *Cristina Branco* (2001) Post-Scriptum

BEST LIVE FADO
> Clube de Fado (p73)
> Parreirinha de Alfama (p75)
> Porta d'Alfama (p72)
> Mesa de Frades (p75)
> A Baîuca (p73)

ARCHITECTURE

From towering Moorish fortifications to sci-fi glass temples, Lisbon's architectural landscape is an extraordinary mix of old and new. Though the city rocked and rolled in the 1755 earthquake, it escaped the WWII bombings that shattered other European capitals to smithereens.

Cracking the spine on Lisbon's history book, you'll revisit Roman times at the 2000-year-old theatre ruins of Museu do Teatro Romano (p68). Flicking forward a millennium brings you to hilltop Castelo de São Jorge (p65), fortified by Moors then besieged by crusaders in 1147, and the kasbah-like Alfama (p64), whose tangle of narrow alleys never became rubble because they were built on bedrock.

In the gripping Manueline chapter, Vasco da Gama discovers India in 1498 and Manuel I pours newfound wealth into Diogo de Boitaca's inventiveness. Mosteiro dos Jerónimos (p80) and Torre de Belém (p81) are Manueline stunners, dripping with organic detail in their coiled stone ropes, twisting columns and weblike vaulting.

Marquês de Pombal rolls up his sleeves in the aftermath of the 1755 earthquake and revamps Lisbon's cityscape with ruler-straight lines, seismic-proof edifices and functional aesthetics. His progressive vision shows in the gridlike streets of Baixa (p52) and monumental squares such as Praça da Figueira (p54) and arcaded Praça do Comércio (p54).

Ah, but this story isn't over yet. Born-again Parque das Nações is a hotbed of design with futuristic glass-and-steel temples from Santiago Calatrava's Gare do Oriente (p90) to Peter Chermayeff's Oceanário (p91). Meanwhile, down by the river, warehouses are morphing into futuristic clubs and restaurants including Lux (p75) and spacey Bica do Sapato (p70).

BEST CLASSIC ICONS
> Mosteiro dos Jerónimos (p80)
> Castelo de São Jorge (p65)
> Igreja de São Vincente da Fora (p65)
> Sé Cathedral (p69)
> Aqueduto das Águas Livres (p100)

BEST CUTTING-EDGE
> Gare do Oriente (p90)
> Pavilhão Atlântico (p96)
> Oceanário (p91)
> Bica do Sapato (p70)
> Centro Cultural de Belém (p86)

MUSEUMS

If Lisbon's sensational museums and galleries have sidestepped the world spotlight, it's because this city prefers to whisper about its charms. Yet it has quietly been hoarding heritage and fine art with a magpielike obsession for decades. Brilliantly curated, eclectic and rarely crowded, its museums showcase Rembrandt oils and fancy baroque carriages that would even make Paris and London swoon.

Lisbon's cultural Matterhorn is Museu Calouste Gulbenkian (p101), an avalanche of Egyptian mummy masks, Renoir paintings and René Lalique sparklers. Next door, Centro de Arte Moderna (p100) presents contemporary masterpieces by Paula Rego and Anthony Gormley. Other peaks include the sublime national gallery Museu Nacional de Arte Antiga (p113), whose rich collection stretches from Dürer originals to bejewelled chalices. Belém's free Museu Colecção Berardo (p80) shows pop stars like Warhol and Lichtenstein, while vaulted Museu do Chiado (p40) lures art buffs with Rodin sculptures and progressive exhibitions.

Astoundingly lovely museums specific to Lisbon feature Museu Nacional dos Coches (p81), housing Cinderella-esque golden coaches, Museu de Marinha (p80) circumnavigating the Age of Discovery with cannonballs and barges, and Museu do Oriente (p113) opening a fascinating window on Asia. MUDE (p54), Lisbon's Museu do Design, will be the new design kid on Baixa's block from late 2009.

BEST CULTURAL KICKS
> Museu do Oriente (p113)
> Museu Nacional do Azulejo (p68)
> Museu de Artes Decorativas (p68)
> Museu Nacional dos Coches (p81)
> Museu de Marinha (p80)

BEST ART HIGHS
> Museu Colecção Berardo (p80)
> Museu Nacional de Arte Antiga (p113)
> Museu Calouste Gulbenkian (p101)
> Centro de Arte Moderna (p100)
> Museu do Chiado (p40)

SNAPSHOTS

NIGHTLIFE

With a live-to-party attitude, twinkling skylines to rival San Francisco and megaclubs hot on Berlin's heels, Lisbon is a must on Europe's nightlife circuit. Bairro Alto offers a Cinders-in-reverse experience with postmidnight bar crawls, while dockside warehouses have been reincarnated as pulsating clubs. Hit Príncipe Real for gay-friendly haunts, Alfama for lantern-lit romance and fado, or Cais do Sodré for loud, sweaty gigs.

Bairro Alto is like an 18-year-old at a house party: hyperactive, touchy-feely and completely smashed. Revellers slam tequilas, bootylicious 20-somethings sway to R 'n' B and everyone spills onto the street with plastic cups of Sagres and beery grins. Work on your *ressaca* (hangover) with *caipirinhas* at Portas Largas (p49). Down the hill, Santa Catarina serves an edgier vibe at beanbag-filled indie den Bicaense (p48), while Music Box (p50) rocks with DJs and emerging bands.

Around 3am, the first clubbers shuffle down to the waterfront. If you only 'do' one club in Lisbon, make it John Malkovich's ultracool Lux (p75), where superstar DJs pump out house and electro to revellers until the first rays glint off the Rio Tejo. Doca de Alcântara's clubbing heavyweights are Kapital (p119) for hot garage and oriental-style Kremlin (p119) for deep house. Dress glam and join a group to slip past the bouncers.

Seeking a low-key vibe? Try stylish Cinco Lounge (p48) for award-winning cocktails and conversing, low-beamed Solar do Vinho do Porto (p49) for vintage port and Pavilhão Chinês (p49) for its Aladdin's cave of kitsch. For top-of-Lisbon views at twilight, relax on the terrace at Noobai Café (p49).

BEST BARS
> Noobai Café (p49)
> Bicaense (p48)
> Cinco Lounge (p48)
> Pavilhão Chinês (p49)
> Portas Largas (p49)

BEST CLUBS
> Music Box (p50)
> Frágil (p50)
> Kapital (p119)
> Kremlin (p119)
> Lux (p75)

AZULEJOS

Suffusing the everyday with vibrant colours and patterns, *azulejos* (tiles), taking their name from the Arabic *az-zulayj* (polished stone), are all over Lisbon – from metro stations to cloisters, beer halls to hostels. Manuel I first brought *azulejos* to Lisbon from Seville in the 15th century.

Museu Nacional do Azulejo (p68) presents a chronological romp of *azulejos* from geometric designs to Renaissance hunting and rococo pastoral scenes. Other golden oldies include Islamic-style *azulejos* at Palácio Nacional de Sintra (p124), diamond-tip majolica at Igreja de São Roque (p37) and blue-and-white gems at Setúbal's Igreja de Jesús (p123). Igreja de São Vicente da Fora (p65) showcases exquisite 18th-century *azulejos* depicting La Fontaine's fables of sly foxes and greedy wolves.

About town, you'll find dazzling electric-blue façades in Bairro Alto, unfussy Pombaline creations in Baixa and the trompe l'oeil marvel Casa do Ferreira das Tabuletas (p62) in Chiado. Quaff a beer while admiring season-inspired *azulejos* at Cervejaria Trindade (p45), then stop by Fábrica Sant'Anna (p41), *azulejo* masters since 1741, to add some porcelain pizzazz to your home.

Go underground to the metro for contemporary *azulejos*, where creatives from Maria Keil to Friedensreich Hundertwasser have revived the art form. Head-turners include critters at zoo-themed Jardim Zoológico, juicy fruits at Laranjeiras (literally 'orange trees') and the white rabbit from *Alice in Wonderland* doing the hop at Cais do Sodré. Parque reveals Age of Discovery themes, Cidade Universitária an erudite mix of owls and philosophers, and Campo Pequeno charging bulls. Gare do Oriente (p90) is the fairest of them all.

BEST TIMELESS AZULEJOS
> Museu Nacional do Azulejo (p68)
> Palácio Nacional de Sintra (p124)
> Igreja de São Vicente da Fora (p65)
> Igreja de São Roque (p37)
> Fábrica Sant'Anna (p41)

BEST METRO TRAILBLAZERS
> Gare do Oriente
> Campo Grande
> Cais do Sodré
> Cidade Universitária
> Campo Pequeno

FOOTBALL

Lisboetas are nuts about *futebol* (football). It's hardly surprising given the strength of their two main rival teams: SL Benfica or *os águias* (the eagles) and Sporting Clube de Portugal aka *os leões* (the lions).

But though the footy is great on Lisbon's home turf, it's the national team that has the Midas touch. Coming fourth in the FIFA World Cup 2006 and reaching the quarter final in Euro 2008, Portugal delivers a scintillating performance. The team's brilliant players includes Benfica's Nuno Gomes and Chelsea's Deco, but golden wonder Cristiano Ronaldo eclipses them all with speed, agility and trickery. At Sporting, he was nicknamed *abelinha* (little bee) until he buzzed off to Manchester United in 2003.

Lisbon's stadiums were given a multimillion euro facelift to host Euro 2004 and the atmosphere at matches is sensational. SL Benfica's hallowed turf is Estádio da Luz (p108; see photo below), where an eagle circles the stadium to land on the club shield at the start of every match. No less impressive is state-of-the-art Estádio José Alvalade, home to Sporting Clube de Portugal (p108). It's worth seeing Os Belenenses at Belém's Estádio do Restelo (p86) for the incredible river views alone, especially from the west stand.

The season runs from September to mid-June, with most league matches on Sunday. Tickets cost around €20 to €55 and are sold at the stadium on match day. For match info and scores, click onto www.afut ebollisboa.org and www.abola.pt (in Portuguese), or for the lowdown in English try www.portuguesesoccer.com and www.portugoal.net.

GREEN LISBON

Lisbon is greener than you might think. Granted, its parks are rarely pond-and-two-bench jobs – instead you'll unearth palm-fringed oases, *praças* (plazas) where fountains gurgle, verdant *miradouros* (viewpoints) and botanical gardens luxuriant with tropical foliage. Wherever you amble, there's a whiff of Portugal's former colonies in the ubiquitous swaying palms, banyan trees and billowing purple jacaranda.

When temperatures soar, get out and stride the ever-so-British Parque Eduardo VII (p101), with its neatly clipped box hedges and skyline views. Other park-pleasers include Jardim da Estrela (p112), flecked with willows, chestnut trees and ponds. The riverfront Parque das Nações is home to Jardim Garcia de Orta (p90), nurturing species from Brazilian silk-cotton trees to Madeiran dragon trees, and splashy boardwalk Caminho da Água (p90). Squares from the cedar-shaded Praça do Príncipe Real to leafy Praça da Alegria (p40) reveal surprising lushness.

Lisbon's botanical gems feature Belém's Jardim do Ultramar (p80), filled with rustling bamboo and lofty date palms. Stroll past ferns, cacti and grottoes in the Estufas (glasshouses; p100), or stretch your limbs in the granddaddy of Lisbon's gardens, 18th-century Jardim Botânico da Ajuda (p82) with its symmetrical parterre and greenhouses brimming with orchids. Sintra (p124) is a classic sylvan beauty, offering vast stretches of pine-brushed and boulder-speckled woodlands.

BEST GREEN HEIGHTS
> Miradouro de São Pedro de Alcântara (p40)
> Miradouro de Santa Catarina (p40)
> Miradouro de Santa Luzia (p65)
> Parque Eduardo VII (p101)
> Quinta da Regaleira (p124)

BEST BOTANICAL ESCAPES
> Jardim da Estrela (p112)
> Jardim do Ultramar (p80)
> Jardim Botânico da Ajuda (p82)
> Estufas (p100)
> Jardim Botânico (p100)

V

SNAPSHOTS

BULLFIGHTING

Nothing in Lisbon sparks as much controversy as *tauromaquia* (bullfighting). In 2006 the neo-Moorish, 9000-seat Campo Pequeno (p107) bullring reopened after six years to the joy of some and frustration of others. Thursday nights from Easter to October, the square heaves with excited spectators and vociferous banner-waving protesters.

Full of pomp and regalia, the *tourada* (bullfight) comprises three parts. First up is the *cavaleiro* (horseman), in glittering 18th-century finery and plumed tricorn, who gracefully parades on a Lusitano to riotous applause and demented, circuslike music. Suddenly, there's a metallic clank and the *touro* (bull) enters. With a ballerina's grace and jockey's strength, the *cavaleiro* shimmies within inches of the bull, stabbing it with barbed *bandarilhas* (spears); as each draws blood, the crowd cheers and the band plays. Enter the *bandarilheiros* (footmen) who provoke the often visibly weakened bull with a pink cape. Finally, it's the turn of the *forcados,* eight foolhardy men who grab the bull by the horns in the *pega* (catch). The suffering bull is led out with the herd and the audience showers the *cavaleiro* with bouquets.

Love it or loathe it, bullfighting is a national institution and popular public event. It's often described as bloodless when compared with bullfighting in other countries, because of a Portuguese law that prohibits killing the animal in public (it's slaughtered later, out of the public eye). However, many animal lovers feel bullfighting is barbaric, immoral and *não é arte nem cultura* (neither art nor culture), and bullfights are met with opposition from animal-welfare organisations, including the Portuguese animal-welfare association (www.lpda.pt), and Animal (www.animal.org.pt), which holds weekly demonstrations.

KIDS

Little things spark kids' imaginations in Lisbon: from rickety rides on bee-yellow trams to traffic-light-bright *pipocas* (popcorn). Easygoing Lisboetas are geared up for families: expect half-price tickets for kids at attractions, half portions (*uma meia dose*) at child-friendly bistros and free transport for under-fives. Hotels often squeeze in cots for tots at no extra charge. Cobbles aren't stroller-friendly, but whizzy funiculars make getting around child's play.

First up for families should be Parque das Nações (p88), where sharks give nippers a toothy grin at the eye-popping Oceanário (p91). Budding physicists launch rockets and become moonwalkers at the touchy-feely Pavilhão do Conhecimento (p91), then cool off at the splashy Jardins d'Água (p90). Head west to dig for nautical treasures in Belém's barge-stuffed Museu de Marinha (p80).

Back in the centre, Castelo de São Jorge (p65) is a surefire hit, as is the Museu da Marioneta (p112), where kids can try their hand at puppetry. Even am-I-bovvered teens perk up shopping Bairro Alto's way cool boutiques like Sneakers Delight (p44) and Agência 117 (p41).

Phew, Lisbon too hot to handle? Kids love making finned friends on dolphin-watching boat rides in Setúbal (p123), burying dad in the sand in Cascais (p126) and fairy-tale play in the palaces and gardens of Sintra (p124).

BEST ATTRACTIONS
> Oceanário (p91)
> Pavilhão do Conhecimento (p91)
> Museu da Marioneta (p112)
> Museu de Marinha (p80)
> Dolphin-watching in Setúbal (p123)

BEST OUTDOORS
> Jardins d'Água (p90)
> Parque Eduardo VII (p101)
> Jardim da Estrela (p112)
> Praça do Príncipe Real (p40)
> Jardim do Ultramar (p80)

GAY & LESBIAN

Increasingly liberal Lisbon harbours a thriving gay and lesbian scene. Portugal was one of the first countries in Europe to ban anti-gay discrimination in 2004 and today gay and lesbian couples enjoy the same legal rights as straights.

The rainbow flag flies high around Praça do Príncipe Real (Map pp38-9), home to a pick 'n' mix of laid-back bars like Bar Água No Bico (p51) and Bar 106 (p51), plus cruisy, hands-on nightspots such as Trumps (p51) and lesbian favourite Memorial (p51). The square itself is a gay cruising mecca.

Chiado and Bairro Alto are also in the pink with gay-friendly (or straight-friendly!) bars, restaurants and boutiques. Kick back with coffee at industrial-cool Mar Adentro (p46) or dinner at the fabulously camp Pap'Açorda (p46). After dark, gays and straights party together with *caipirinhas* at Portas Largas (p49) and house anthems at pulsating Frágil (p50), before hitting the riverfront for hedonistic clubbing at Kremlin (p119) or Lux (p75). Bed-down at Bairro Alto's gay hotel Anjo Azul (www.anjoazul.com).

Plan your visit to catch Lisbon Pride (p25) in June and gay flicks at the Festival de Cinema Gay e Lésbico (p26) in September. For gay event listings, click onto www.portugalgay.pt, www.ilga-portugal.pt and http://timeout.sapo.pt (in Portuguese).

BEST CLUBS
> Frágil (p50)
> Lux (p75)
> Trumps (p51)
> Kremlin (p119)
> Kapital (p119)

BEST BARS
> Bar Água No Bico (p51)
> Bric-a-Bar (p51)
> Bar 106 (p51)
> Portas Largas (p49)

>BACKGROUND

Fransisco de Arruda's 1515 Manueline flight-of-fancy – Torre de Belém (p81)

BACKGROUND

HISTORY

Imperial riches, fires, plague, Europe's worst recorded earthquake, revolutions, coups and a dictatorship – Lisbon's history reads like the script for a blockbuster thriller. And you can literally go backstage: whether treading cobbles in the Moorish Alfama (p64), marvelling at Marquês de Pombal's 18th-century handiwork in Baixa (p52) or revisiting the Age of Discovery in time capsule Belém (p78). Lisbon's tale is laced with adventure and edge-of-your-seat moments.

ROMAN ROOTS & MOORISH ROCKS

The Phoenicians pipped other civilisations to the post 3000 years ago, but it wasn't until the Romans arrived in 205 BC that Lisbon, or Olissippo, really took root. Julius Caesar made it the western capital of the Roman Empire in 60 BC and the municipium thrived on fish-preserving industries. The remains of a theatre at Museu do Teatro Romano (p68) flash back to Roman times.

After some tribal chaos, Lisbon was taken over by North African Moors in 711. They fortified the city they called Lissabona, building the high-and-mighty Castelo de São Jorge (p65), and did a remarkable job of fending off the Christians for 400 years. Lisbon flourished as a trade centre under Moorish rule and they were a tolerant bunch, allowing Jews and Christians to practise their faith as long as they coughed up their taxes. Wander through the medina-like Alfama (p64) for a taste of Moorish Lisbon.

But after the four-month Siege of Lisbon in 1147, Christian fighters (mainly British crusader hooligan-pillagers) under King Afonso Henriques finally managed to recapture the city and banish the Moors. To demonstrate their superior power, they erected fortified Sé cathedral (p69) above the ruins of the main mosque in 1150. In 1260 Afonso III moved his capital here from Coimbra, a strategic move given the city's excellent port and central position.

AGE OF EMPIRES

The Age of Discovery began in earnest in the 15th century when explorers, eager to break the Venetian monopoly on overland trade with Asia, set sail aboard mighty caravels. Among the first at the helm was Prince Henry the

Navigator whose men discovered Madeira (1419) and the Azores (1427), and who himself washed up on West African shores. Vasco da Gama (p81) discovered a sea route to India in 1498 and – in historical terms – a few nautical miles later Pedro Álvares Cabral's fleet reached Brazil (1500).

In the 16th century, often hailed Portugal's Golden Age, life was very rosy indeed. Colonising, coffers laden with sugar, spices and gold, and the altogether less savoury business of slave trade proved highly lucrative. Lisbon looked well on it, with King Manuel I (r 1495–1521) flaunting his newfound wealth in exuberant Manueline architecture like Mosteiro dos Jerónimos (p80). Their appetites were insatiable and, by 1571, Portugal had a huge slice of the global pie with outposts all the way to Nagasaki, Japan.

But Portugal didn't keep its monopoly grip for long. Imperial rivals Britain, France, Spain and Holland joined the colony race and competition was fierce. Spain laid claim to Portugal in 1580 and kept a stranglehold until 1668, when the Peace Treaty of Lisbon ended 29 years of bloody wars and restored Portuguese rule. Meanwhile, Portugal was losing imperial weight and Brazil's independence in 1822 dealt a particularly heavy blow. Try as Salazar would to keep the colonial ship afloat in the 20th century, it was sinking fast. Macau, Portugal's last colony, was returned to China in 1999.

MOVERS & SHAKERS

At 9.40am on All Saints' Day, 1 November 1755, a violent earthquake hit Lisbon, measuring a stratospheric 9.0 on the Richter scale. The tremors brought an even more devastating fire and a tsunami with reverberations as far as Agadir. Estimates suggest that as many as 90,000 of Lisbon's 270,000 inhabitants died. The city lay almost totally in ruins. Immediately, King João I's chief minister, the formidable Marquês de Pombal, began to pick up the pieces and rebuild Lisbon. His gridlike streets and functional, earthquake-proof buildings were incredibly advanced; Baixa (p52) is a prime example.

Napoleon's forces occupied the city from 1807 to 1811 and Lisbon slid into chaos: property was plundered and the royal family fled to Brazil. By mid-century, the country was flourishing under Maria II, whose passion for pretty palaces included Sintra's whimsical 1840 Palácio Nacional da Pena (p124). A mushrooming Lisbon needed room to breathe and in 1879 the capital was extended north via the grand, Parisian-style Avenida da Liberdade (Map p99). By the turn of the century, Lisbon's trams began to operate.

FLOWER POWER

April 25 1974, marked a turning point in Lisbon's history when army officers overthrew the regime by leading an almost bloodless, leftist coup. The revolutionaries used no force. Persuaded by a carnation-waving public to proceed peacefully, soldiers placed red carnations – a symbol of love and affection – in their rifle barrels; hence the name Carnation Revolution (Revolução dos Cravos). The bridge named after Salazar was rebaptised Ponte 25 de Abril (p114). At long last, Portugal was free of its dictatorial shackles and paving the way for democracy. The revolution is remembered on April 25 or Freedom Day (Dia da Liberdade).

MONARCHY FALLS, SALAZAR RISES

The early 20th century meant troubled times for Lisbon. In 1908 King Carlos and his eldest son were assassinated in Praça do Comércio. Then a revolution on 5 October 1910 forced King Manuel II to abdicate and the Primeira República (First Republic) was established. Political ground was shaky, inflation spiralled and in 1926 a coup d'état brought General Antonio de Fragoso Carmona to power, marking the start of Portugal's dictatorship.

António de Oliveira Salazar filled his shoes as prime minister of the Estado Novo (New State) in 1932. A devout Roman Catholic, Salazar led an authoritarian, right-wing regime, backing Franco's nationalists in the 1936 Spanish Civil War. The Policia Internacional e de Defesa do Estado (PIDE), Portugal's Gestapo-style secret police, weeded out and eliminated communists and insurgents. In WWII he steered Portugal down a middle road. Though officially neutral, he turned a blind eye to the spies in Lisbon and allowed Allies to use air bases in the Azores.

Salazar's primary concern was monetary stability and this he achieved by keeping an iron-handed grip on the colonies. He shocked the world in the 1960s by using infantry and militia to quell dissidents in colonial Africa. Never fully recovering from a stroke in 1968, he died in 1970. Marcelo Caetano took his place until the regime was finally overthrown in 1974, paving the way for democracy. In 1974 and 1975 there was a massive influx of refugees from the former African colonies, changing Lisbon's demographic and adding to its richness culturally, if not financially.

LIFE AS A LISBOETA

So who exactly are Lisboetas? Believe the clichés and you'll have them down as conservative Catholics, still munching sardines, wallowing in

SOCIAL GRACES

> Do say *bom dia* (morning) or *boa tarde* (afternoon) when entering shops and cafes.
> Do sing the praises of local food, culture and heritage.
> Do break the ice by rattling off names of famous Portuguese football stars like Cristiano Ronaldo.
> Do address older people with *Senhor* (Mr) and *Senhora* (Mrs).
> Do try to speak Portuguese, however clumsily – they'll love you for it.
> Don't talk, whisper or fidget when a fado singer is giving it her all.
> Don't queue jump.
> Don't assume Lisboetas speak Spanish. If in doubt, ask *fala espanhol?*
> Don't jaywalk unless you want to test locals' honking and swearing ability.
> Don't take opening times literally. Many places open, well, when they feel like it.

saudade (nostalgic longing), bemoaning colonial losses, and obsessed with the big three: fado, football and Fátima. Despite huge progress since shrugging off its Salazar straightjacket and leapfrogging into the EU, there's no denying Lisbon had an image problem until recently: seen as the shabbier, shyer and altogether less sexy girl-next-door of flamboyant extrovert Spain.

Not any more. Urban regeneration, multicultural flavour and a wave of new creativity are giving gen-X Lisboetas plenty to smile about and newfound confidence. By nature they are more demure than the Spanish, but their *festas* (parties) are just as pumping, and they're more likely to be sleeping off a *caipirinha* hangover Sunday mornings than attending church nowadays. Historic buildings are being revamped, funky bars and restaurants are spreading like wildfire, life quality is up, tourism booming. Lisbon's transformation has been dramatic: from Sandra Dee to Pink Lady in less than a decade.

On one hand, the city moves at a relaxed, almost dreamlike, pace, particularly in stuck-in-time districts such as Alfama and Belém. You'll nearly always get a seat on the metro, city dwellers rarely rush and most restaurants will squeeze you in at the last minute. Perhaps it's the Atlantic breeze, the light bouncing of the Tejo, the fact you can eat alfresco – and afford to – or simply that this is one of Europe's mildest cities (3300 hours of sunshine a year) that makes Lisbon seem genetically programmed to move slower than other EU capitals. It's refreshing.

Yet don't be fooled into thinking Lisbon is just a collection of pastel-washed, old-world villages. If Lisboetas seem to be lazily recharging their

LIGHTEN UP

Portugal's smoking ban came into force on 1 January 2008, allowing nonsmokers to breathe easier in public buildings, workplaces, theatres and museums. But as with many things, the rules are more relaxed in Lisbon than in other European capitals. As long as they install proper ventilation systems, bars, clubs and restaurants under 100 sq m can still allow punters to puff away. Ironically, António Nunes, head of the Portuguese Food Standards Agency and man behind the new legislation, was caught (illegally) lighting up in a casino on New Year's Day. As we said, more relaxed...

batteries during the day, it's because they need their energy for the *noite* (night). Hedonistic, decadent, call them what you will, young Lisboetas love to socialise and embrace life to the blurry-eyed fullest; whether they're sharing plastic cups of Sagres on Bairro Alto's streets or sweet-talking their way into Lux at 4am. And the more the merrier. Lisboetas are open and nonjudgemental, so you'll make friends quickly, especially if you *fala um pouco de português* (speak a little Portuguese).

Conservative? Hmmm, maybe superficially, but below the surface you'll find an egalitarian, largely machismo-free society. Lisbon's split personality means one month it's celebrating saints with feasting and the next gay pride with fervour. Lisboetas aren't obsessed with status and wealth, either, with individual style trumping designer wear any day. As one local put it so beautifully, they are 'lovers of simple and constant pleasures', generally happy with their lot and just as happy with kerbside tapas as Michelin-starred finery.

Young Lisboetas are often cultured, creative and tech-savvy, but as these qualities are mixed with an earthy authenticity and a genuine inquisitiveness about other countries and languages, they rarely come across as being arrogant. Tired of playing second fiddle to other European capitals, Lisboetas are striking up their own 21st-century symphony: a composition of past melancholy and future brilliance, two worlds that happily coexist here. It deserves a standing ovation.

ENVIRONMENT

Organic may not be a buzzword yet, but Lisbon is quietly staging its own green revolution. Locals have woken up to the virtues of recycling, installing public bins to separate waste. And they've cottoned on to carbon-neutral transport, too. Take a stroll through Baixa and you'll see

GREEN GROW THE RUSHES, O

Ever shall it be so at Mata de Sesimbra, a groundbreaking ecotourism project 30km south of Lisbon. Part of the One Planet Living challenge and brainchild of WWF (www.panda .org) and BioRegional (www.bioregional.com), this zero-waste and zero-carbon community will turn the tide on an area once infamous for heavy quarrying and coastal erosion. When completed in around 2014 at the cost of a cool €1 billion, the 30,000-strong community will be a shining example of sustainable living. Here's the deal: homes, shops, offices and leisure facilities using renewable energy, hybrid eco-shuttles to eliminate carbon emissions, 50% of food sourced locally to revive agriculture and fisheries, and wastewater recycling to cut the consumption of precious resources. It will also be Europe's biggest-ever nature restoration scheme, with 4800 hectares of a total 5300 being given over to restoring wetlands, enhancing biodiversity and reforesting native pine and oak forests.

ecoconscious cops zipping around on Segways, battery-operated, nonpolluting scooters. Baby steps, sure, but they're heading in the right direction.

One thing that always strikes first-timers in Lisbon is its smog-free, dazzling blue sky. Not without reason is the air so pure. Efficient and affordable public transport has significantly reduced congestion and carbon emissions; trams are fun, buses frequent, the metro speedy, so why take the car? Lisbon's topography is also such that certain bits can only be reached on foot – from the twisting steps of Alfama and Graça to the pedestrianised Baixa – so you'll keep fit and do your bit for the environment. The seaside playground of Cascais (p126) has freewheeled into the picture recently by offering free bike rental.

Lisbon is also revamping urban landscapes. Standouts include Parque das Nações (p88), which has morphed from a polluting, oil-refining monster to an ecotrailblazer in less than a decade. Gone are the factories and in their place are energy efficient glass-and-steel temples. A similar story is the regeneration of Doca de Alcântara (p110), whose industrial warehouses are getting a new lease of life as hip bars and restaurants. All in the quest for a cleaner, greener Lisbon.

ETHNIC LISBON

Lisbon, locals will proudly tell you, is a multicultural city: there are Mozambican football players, Goan restaurants and *rodas de choro* (Brazilian jam sessions). It's true, Greater Lisbon accommodates around 120,000 people of Asian, African and Brazilian descent and their cultures permeate every aspect of society – from food and music to TV and street slang. Many came to Lisbon after the 1974 revolution, *retornados* (returned ones) from countries like Cape Verde, Mozambique, Guinea-Bissau and war-torn Angola; a move that placed huge pressure on Portugal's fragile economy.

And yet, when you then ask Lisboetas where most of these people actually are, they will tell you with genuine regret 'in the ghettos'. There is a whole Lisbon out there that the brochures don't talk about: Cova da Moura, Fontainhas, Anjos, Amadora, Buraca…suburbs most people won't venture into that you suddenly glimpse through the window on the train to Sintra. They are a far cry from picture-postcard Lisbon with their cramped shanty houses, drug-related violence and high teenage pregnancy rates. Young Lisboetas here lack prospects and are often in cultural limbo which is, of course, only exacerbated by tabloid headlines reinforcing stereotypes, using them as scapegoats and badmouthing the *clandestinos* (illegal immigrants).

Social services are addressing these issues, but there's still a way to go. No-go areas even for streetwise locals, these districts are the frayed edges of Lisbon's social fabric. Films like Pedro Costa's *Bones* (opposite) provide an excellent insight into a side of Lisbon that is, sadly, often overlooked and forgotten.

FURTHER READING

A Small Death in Lisbon (2000; Robert Wilson) An intelligent and compelling thriller that juxtaposes worn-torn Europe with modern-day Lisbon when an inspector unravels dark facts about the murder of a girl.

Lovers in Lisbon (1988; Barbara Cartland) A wonderfully clichéd romance by the hearts-and-flowers Dame. One for the plane…

Night Train to Lisbon (2008; Pascal Mercier) This dreamlike story tells of a Swiss teacher's soul-searching journey to Lisbon in the 1930s.

The Company of Strangers (2002; Robert Wilson) Gripping, well-developed thriller evolving in wartime Lisbon, a hotbed of espionage.

The Great Shadow (1915; Mário de Sá-Carneiro) Crazy, ingenious and surreal collection of short stories by Sá-Carneiro, a friend of Fernando Pessoa.

The History of the Siege of Lisbon (História de Cerco de Lisboa; 2000; José Saramago) Nobel Prize winner Saramago's ingenious and imaginative tale is about a proofreader who rewrites the history of the 1147 Siege of Lisbon by inserting a negative into a sentence.

The Journal of a Voyage to Lisbon (1755; Henry Fielding) English novelist Fielding's posthumously published diary of his tortuous 1754 voyage to Lisbon in a vain attempt to recover his health. He is buried in Cemitério dos Ingleses (p112).

THE PEOPLE'S POET

'Wise is he who enjoys the show offered by the world', said Lisbon's best-loved 19th-century poet Fernando Pessoa (1888–1935). After his father died from tuberculosis, Fernando was shipped over to South Africa and educated in English, where the bright spark devoured Dickens and Shakespeare. Upon his return, he penned poetry for forward-thinking magazines such as *Orpheu*. His poems reveal themes of *saudosismo* (nostalgic longing), tedium, mystical patriotism and general disgust for life. The esoteric poem *Mensagem* (Message; 1934) was the only complete work published in his lifetime. Today the poet's face graces souvenirs from kitschy cork placemats to T-shirts. If you want a better insight into Pessoa's work, grab a copy of his verse and take a pew next to his bronze statue on the terrace at A Brasileira (p47).

The Lusiads (Os Lusíadas; 1572; Luís Vaz de Camões) This epic poem in Homeric style recounts Vasco da Gama's 1497 voyage to India and encapsulates the spirit of Portugal's Age of Discovery.
The Night in Lisbon (1998; Erich Maria Remarque) An evocative and harrowing perspective on WWII Europe, as seen through the eyes of refugees attempting to flee Lisbon.
Travels in my Homeland (Viagens na Minha Terra; 1846; Almeida Garrett) Hybrid of fact and fiction recounting Garrett's journey from Lisbon to Santarém, interwoven with the dilemma of a man torn between two lovers.
Winter in Lisbon (1999; Antonio Muñoz Molina) Touching portrayal of a US jazz pianist who finds rhythm and love in Lisbon.

FILMS

A Talking Picture (Um Filme Falado; 2004; Manoel de Oliveira) For some thought-provoking, for others dull – this movie reveals the encounters of a mother and daughter on a Mediterranean cruise. John Malkovich is the captain.
Bones (Ossos; 1997; Pedro Costa) A grim and gripping tale of life in the slums on the outskirts of Lisbon, dealing with poverty, suicide and the struggle of love and death.
Christopher Columbus – The Enigma (Cristóvão Colombo; 2007; Manoel de Oliveira) Christopher Columbus Italian? Not necessarily. A researcher sets out to prove that he could be Portuguese in this melancholic, rewrite-the-history-books feature.
In Vanda's Room (No Quarto da Vanda; 2000; Pedro Costa) This award-winning, warts-and-all documentary/fiction provides a close-up of the lives of Cape Verdean slum dwellers and drug addicts in Lisbon's deprived Fontainhas district.
Lisbon Story (Viagem a Lisboa; 1994; Wim Wenders) Inventive and beautifully photographed, this German drama follows director Monroe on his quest to finish a silent film in Lisbon. Stars Portuguese band Madredeus and a cameo by Manoel de Oliveira.
The Letter (A Carta; 1999; Manoel de Oliveira) Passion, futile love, adultery, tragedy, piety...it's all in this Oliveira classic that won the Jury prize at Cannes.

DON'T STOP ME NOW…

It certainly seems there's no stopping cinema centenarian Manoel de Oliveira from defying the laws of longevity. Born in Porto in 1908 and frequently cited as the world's oldest active director, the highly acclaimed film-maker began his prolific career in the silent movie era and has since directed some 50 features, documentaries and shorts, achieving epic weight in *Voyage to the Beginning of the World* and *The Letter*. His films range from obscure to self-reflexive, revealing themes from morality struggles to childhood rediscovery. In 2008 Cannes and the Brooklyn Academy of Music are paying homage to a man who has increased his creative output with age. Well he always was a bit of a maverick…

The Mutants (Os Mutantes; 1999; Teresa Villaverde) Nominated for four Golden Globes, this bleak drama sparked nationwide controversy. It focuses on four teenagers rejected by the system, who fall into a life of petty crime and pornography.

The Winter in Lisbon (El Invierno en Lisboa; 1992; Jose Antonio Zorrilla) This crime drama is about a disillusioned US jazz pianist who flees to Lisbon where he befriends an artist. Stars famous trumpet player Dizzy Gillespie.

Voyage to the Beginning of the World (Viagem ao Princípio do Mundo; 1997; Manoel de Oliveira) This brilliantly cast Fipresci Award winner is a moving, insightful portrayal of childhood rediscovered on a road trip through rural Portugal.

DIRECTORY
TRANSPORT
ARRIVAL & DEPARTURE
AIR

Direct flights to Lisbon depart frequently from hubs including London, Barcelona, Paris, New York and Berlin. Situated about 7km north of central Lisbon, the ultramodern **Aeroporto de Lisboa** (Lisbon Airport; ☎ 218 413 500; www .ana.pt) is served by international carriers such as Lufthansa, British Airways and TAP Portugal, plus budget airlines like easyJet and bmibaby. Head to terminal 1 for international flights and terminal 2 for domestic departures; a free shuttle links terminals.

Facilities at the airport feature a 24-hour bureau de change, car rental, ATMs, left luggage and international press.

VISA

EU nationals need no visa for any length of stay in Portugal. Visitors from the US, Canada, Australia and New Zealand can stay for up to 90 days in any half-year without a visa. Everyone else needs a visa (unless a spouse or child of an EU citizen).

GETTING AROUND
Pedestrianised streets, twisting alleys and *miradouros* (viewpoints)

Travel to/from the Airport

	Taxi	Bus: AeroBus 91	Bus: 44, 45, 43
Pick-up point	Outside arrivals	Outside arrivals	Outside arrivals
Drop-off point	Anywhere	Stops include Marquês de Pombal, Avenida da Liberdade, Rossio, Praça do Comércio	Stops include Praça dos Restauradores, Cais do Sodré, Amoreiras
Duration	To centre, 20 minutes (30 in rush hour)	To centre, 25 minutes (35 in rush hour)	To centre 35 minutes (45 in rush hour)
Cost	To centre, €10-12	€3.35 day pass	€1.35 one-way
Other	€1.60 charged for luggage	No service 8.15pm to 7.45am daily; otherwise runs every 20 minutes; ticket valid all day on Carris buses and trams	No service 9.30pm to 7pm daily; otherwise run every 10 to 15 minutes; avoid using in rush hour if you have a lot of luggage
Contact	☎ 218 444 050 to prebook cab	www.carris.pt	www.carris.pt

adding altitude to sightseeing make for pleasurable urban ambling in districts like Alfama, Bairro Alto and Baixa. **Carris** (www .carris.pt) operates Lisbon's inexpensive and efficient public transport network except the metro. This guide notes the nearest metro station after Ⓜ , the nearest bus route after the icon 🚌 , and the nearest tram route after 🚃 in each listing.

TRAVEL PASSES

Save with a one-day travel pass (€3.70), offering unlimited travel on all public transport including the metro until midnight. It's available at metro stations. For 50¢, you can buy a 7 Colinas card (similar to London's Oyster card) that you can credit.

METRO

Lisbon's shiny **metro** (☎ 213 500 115; www.metrolisboa.pt) comprises four lines (blue, yellow, red and green). Though it doesn't cover all districts, it's a speedy way to reach Parque das Nações, Marquês de Pombal, Rato and Saldanha. It runs from 6.30am to 1am daily. Single/ return tickets for one/two zones cost €1.25/1.90 and €1.55/2.45. A book of 10 tickets costs €7.40 for one zone and €10.35 for two zones.

TRAM

You can't miss Lisbon's bright yellow trams (eléctricos), operating on five routes (12, 15, 18, 25 and 28). You can buy a ticket (singles cost €1.35) on board, which you should validate in the machine next to the driver. Top routes include 28 (p15), taking in Lisbon's key sights, and 15 from Praça da Figueira to Belém; the former runs roughly every 15 minutes from 6am to 11pm, the latter from 5.45am to 1.15am. There are fewer services on Sundays.

GREEN TRAVEL

In the age of budget airlines, it's easy just to book a flight, but consider swapping fast but polluting aeroplanes for more ecofriendly ways of travelling to Lisbon. Trains may be slower, but you can luxuriate in the journey itself and do your bit for the environment. If you're coming from London, for instance, you could catch the Eurostar to Paris, switch to the high-speed TGV to Irun (on the Spanish border), then board the Sud Express overnight train and arrive in Lisbon in time for a late breakfast. Alternatively, you could travel from Paris to Madrid, spend the day exploring the Spanish capital, then board an overnight sleeper to Lisbon.

For the lowdown on alternative methods of reaching Lisbon click onto www.seat61.com, or find more info and tickets at www.raileurope.com.

CLIMATE CHANGE & TRAVEL

Travel – especially air travel – is a significant contributor to global climate change. At Lonely Planet, we believe that all who travel have a responsibility to limit their personal impact. As a result, we have teamed with Rough Guides and other concerned industry partners to support Climate Care, which allows people to offset the greenhouse gases they are responsible for with contributions to energy-saving projects and other climate-friendly initiatives in the developing world. Lonely Planet offsets all staff and author travel.

For more information, turn to the responsible travel pages on www.lonelyplanet .com. For details on offsetting your carbon emissions and a carbon calculator, go to www .climatecare.org.

BUS

Lisbon's network of 88 buses (autocarros) includes eight night routes. Single tickets costing €1.35 can be bought from the driver. You'll find route maps and timetables at stops. Daytime operation hours vary, night buses run from 11.45pm to 5.30am. Useful routes feature bus 1 (Cais do Sodré to Charneca via Baixa and Avenida da Liberdade), bus 27 (Marquês de Pombal to Belém via Estrela, Lapa and Doca de Alcântara) and night bus 201 (Cais do Sodré to Belém via Doca de Alcântara).

FUNICULAR

Cranking up and down the hills, Lisbon's nostalgic funiculars (elevadores) are great for tired legs. Single tickets cost €1.35. A favourite, and also the steepest, is Elevador da Bica (p37).

TAXI

Lisbon's Mercedes taxis are plentiful and can be booked over the phone, hailed on the street – if they stop – or picked up outside train stations. The fare on the meter should read €2.50 (daytime flag fall). You'll be charged an extra €1.60 for luggage and an additional 20% for journeys between 9pm and 6am. To book a cab, call:
Rádio Táxis (☎ 218 119 000)
Télétaxi (☎ 218 111 100)

TRAIN

Long-distance trains run by Comboios de Portugal (CP) depart from **Santa Apolónia** (Map pp66-7, F3; ☎ 808 208 208; www.cp.pt). The train to Sintra (p124) departs every 20 minutes from Estação do Rossio (Map p53, B2), takes 40 minutes and costs €1.70. Departing from Cais do Sodré (Map pp38–9, D7), the train to Cascais via Estoril (p126) runs every 20 minutes, takes 40 minutes and costs €1.70.

PRACTICALITIES
BUSINESS HOURS

Most shops open from 9.30am to 7pm Monday to Friday and to 1pm Saturday. Bairro Alto boutiques open around 2pm to 10pm or midnight. Malls and department stores usually open from 10am to 11pm. Virtually all shops are closed on Sunday.

Government offices are open from 9am to noon and 2pm to 5pm Monday to Friday, while banks open 8.30am to 3pm Monday to Friday. Restaurants open for lunch from noon to 3pm and dinner from 7pm to 11pm. For late-night dining, try Bairro Alto. Museums usually open from 10am to 6pm and are closed on Monday.

For more information, see Quick Reference on the inside front cover.

DISCOUNTS

If you're planning lots of sight-seeing, the **Lisboa Card** (24/48/72hr adult €15/26/32, under 11yr €8/13/16) represents excellent value. The card offers unlimited use of public transport (including trains to Sintra and Cascais), entry to all key museums and attractions and up to 50% discount on tours. It's available at Ask Me Lisboa tourist offices, including the one at the airport.

Many museums offer 50% discounts for seniors and students and are free for under-sixes. If you're on a budget, visit museums on Sunday mornings when many offer free entry.

ELECTRICITY

Voltage is 220V, 50Hz. Continental-style two-pin plugs are standard.

EMERGENCIES

Overall, Lisbon is a safe city, but you'll probably be offered hashish and back-of-the-truck goods by hawkers in Bairro Alto and Baixa. A firm, polite 'no' should keep them at bay. Mind your wallet at tourist hubs, especially on Rua Augusta and tram 28.

Main streets are relatively safe to walk along at night, though be wary around metro stations such as Anjos, Martim Moniz and In-tendente, where there have been muggings. You should also take care in the dark alleys of Alfama and Graça. Emergency phone numbers:

Ambulance, Fire Brigade, Police (☎ 112)
24hr Pharmacy Info (☎ 118)
24hr Tourist Police (☎ 213 421 634)

HOLIDAYS

New Year's Day (Dia do Ano Novo) 1 January
Shrove Tuesday (Terça-Feira Gorda) February/March
Good Friday (Sexta-Feira Santa) March/April
Easter Monday (Segunda-Feira da Páscoa) March/April
Freedom Day (Dia da Liberdade) 25 April

Labour Day (Dia do Trabalhador) 1 May
Corpus Christi (Corpo de Deus) May/June
National Day (Dia de Camões) 10 June
St Anthony's Day (Festa de Santo António) 13 June
Assumption Day (Dia da Assunção) 15 August
Republic Day (Dia de República) 5 October
All Saint's Day (Dia de Todos-os-Santos) 1 November
Independence Day (Dia da Restauração) 1 December
Immaculate Conception (Imaculada Conceição) 8 December
Christmas Day (Dia de Natal) 25 December

INTERNET

Many cafes and hotels now offer free wi-fi for customers. Otherwise, there are numerous internet cafes in Bairro Alto and Rossio, including inexpensive ones around Largo de São Domingos (Map p53, B2), which charge €1 to €1.50 per hour. If you don't use all your time, save your ticket to log in again. Parque das Nações is a wi-fi hotspot. To search for others, click onto www.jiwire.com or www.hotspot-locations.com. Handy Lisbon websites for pretrip planning:

Ask Me Lisboa (www.askmelisboa.com) Multilingual website with info on discount cards.
Câmara Municipal de Lisboa (www.cm-lisboa.pt/turismo) The groovy municipal site with info on upcoming events.
Go Lisbon (www.golisbon.com) Packed with up-to-date info on sightseeing, eating, nightlife and events.
Guia da Noite (www.guiadanoite.com) Upcoming events and nightlife listings.

Lisboa Brighter Place (http://lisboa.brighterplace.com) Fun website with student info on bars and clubs.
Lisbon Tourist Board (www.visitlisboa.com) Lisbon's comprehensive tourism website covers everything from must-sees to transport and accommodation.
Lonely Planet (www.lonelyplanet.com) Information, links and resources.
Time Out Lisboa (http://timeout.sapo.pt) Up-and-coming gigs, cultural happenings and interesting commentary, in Portuguese.
Visit Portugal (www.visitportugal.com) Portugal's official tourism website, covering sights, practicalities and events.

LANGUAGE
BASICS

Hello.	*Bom dia.*
Hi.	*Olá.*
Good afternoon.	*Boa tarde.*
Good evening/night.	*Boa noite.*
Goodbye.	*Adeus.*
Excuse me/Sorry.	*Desculpe.*
See you later.	*Até logo.*
How are you?	*Como está?*
Fine, and you?	*Tudo bem, e tu?*
Yes.	*Sim.*
No.	*Não.*
Please.	*Faz favor.*
Thank you (very much).	*(Muito) obrigado/a.* (m/f)
You're welcome.	*De nada.*
Do you speak English?	*Fala inglês?*
I (don't) understand.	*(Não) entendo.*
How much is it?	*Quanto é?*
That's too expensive.	*É muito caro.*

EATING & DRINKING

I'm vegetarian.	*Sou vegetariano/a.* (m/f)
Can I have the bill/check, please.	*A conta se faz favor.*

Can I see the menu, please?	*Posso ver o menu, por favor?*
Can I see the wine list, please?	*Posso ver a carta de vinhos, por favor?*
A table for…please.	*Uma mesa para…., se faz favor.*

MONEY

Though Lisbon is gradually creeping into line with other EU capitals, your euros will still stretch pretty far. Budget on around €80 to €120 per person, per day, if you're planning on staying in three-star accommodation and eating at midrange places. Luxury lovers desiring the A-list treatment can easily double that figure, while clued-up budget travellers can get by on as little as €40. It's worth bearing in mind that many of Lisbon's *churrasqueiras* (grill houses) offer great-value lunch specials.

ATMs (Multibancos) are the easiest way to access your money, accepting most major cards including Visa, Cirrus and Maestro. Note that Lisbon is not entirely plastic-friendly, with many shops, bistros and even *pensões* (pensions) only accepting cash. For currency exchange rates, see Quick Reference on the inside front cover.

NEWSPAPERS

Lisboetas are a literary lot with several dailies, including thought-provoking *Público* (www.publico .clix.pt), left-leaning *Diário de Notícias* (http://dn.sapo.pt), local-news-oriented *Jornal de Notícias* (http://jn.sapo.pt) and financial biggie *Diario Económico* (http://diarioeconomico.com). Locals get their scandal fix with tabloid *24 Horas* (www.24horasnewspaper .com), while football junkies buy *Bola* (www.abola.pt). Freebies being rustled on the metro on weekdays feature *Metro*, *Global* and *Meia Hora*. *The Resident* (www .portugalresident.com) and *The News* (www.the-news.net) are English-language papers.

ORGANISED TOURS

SPECIALISED TOURS

Naturway (☎ 213 918 090; www.naturway .pt; €50; ☼ 8.30am) Offbeat, four-wheel drive tours of coast and countryside. Full-day excursions include Sintra and Arrábida. Hotel pick-up and drop-off.

Sidecar Touring (☎ 963 965 105; www .sidecartouring.co.pt) These crazy dudes offer sidecar tours ranging from giddying spins of Sintra to night rides over Ponte 25 de Abril. Prices and times vary.

Transtejo (Map p53, D6; ☎ 218 824 671; www.transtejo.pt; Terreiro do Paço ferry terminal; adult/child €20/10; ☼ 3pm Apr-Oct) These 2½-hour river cruises are a laid-back way to enjoy Lisbon's sights. Multilingual commentary.

WALKING TOURS

Lisbon Walker (Map p53, C5; ☎ 218 861 840; www.lisbonwalker.com; Rua dos Remédios 84; 3hr walk adult/under 12yr/under

26yr €15/free/10; ⏰ 10am & 2.30pm) This excellent company, with well-informed, English-speaking guides, offers themed walking tours through Lisbon; they depart from the northeast corner of Praça do Comércio.

Walks on the Art Side (☎ 214 141 055; www.walksontheartside.com; Rua João das Regras; 12) Walks through Lisbon with an arty twist, from Chiado architecture to Belém *azulejos* (tiles). Tours vary in price, time and duration. Meeting points vary, so call ahead for details.

TELEPHONE

Portugal uses the GSM 900/1800 network, compatible with Europe, Australia and most of Asia. Most payphones require a phone card, available in denominations of €3, €6 and €9 at kiosks and newsagents. For long-distance and international calls, it's cheaper to head to one of the discount call shops-cum-cybercafes on Largo de São Domingos (Map p53, B2).

COUNTRY & CITY CODES

Portugal's country code is ☎ 351 and the Lisbon code is ☎ 21. To call abroad from Portugal, dial ☎ 00 before the country code.

USEFUL PHONE NUMBERS

International Directory Inquiries (☎ 177)
National Directory Inquiries (☎ 118)

TIPPING

Service charge *(serviço)* is usually included in restaurant bills and taxi fares, but reward good service with a 10% tip. At restaurants, you'll automatically be brought a basket with bread, butter and pâté, charged per item. If you don't want it, it's fine to say so. Tip porters around €1 per bag.

TOURIST INFORMATION

Ask Me Lisboa Rua Augusta (Map p53, C4; ☎ 213 259 131; ⏰ 10am-1pm & 2-6pm); Santa Apolónia (Map pp66-7, G3; ☎ 218 821 606; inside train station; ⏰ 8am-1pm Wed-Sat); Largo dos Jerónimos (Map p/9, C3; ☎ 213 658 435; ⏰ 10am-1pm & 2-6pm Tue-Sat); Palácio Foz (Map p53, A2; Praça dos Restauradores; ☎ 213 463 314; ⏰ 9am-8pm); Lisbon Airport (☎ 218 450 660; Arrivals; ⏰ 7am-midnight). Turismo de Lisboa runs several info kiosks; these are the most useful.
Lisbon Welcome Centre (Map p53, C5; ☎ 210 312 810; www.visitlisboa.com; Praça do Comércio; ⏰ 9am-8pm) is the main branch of Lisbon tourist board, Turismo de Lisboa, providing free city maps, brochures and hotel and tour booking services. You can buy the Lisboa Card here.

TRAVELLERS WITH DISABILITIES

Lisbon is making steady progress to cater for people with disabilities, though the steep, cobbled lanes of Alfama, Graça and Bairro Alto can be difficult for wheelchair users to negotiate. Districts such as Parque das Nações, Baixa and Belém are more accessible.

Several metro stations have lifts and ticket machines equipped for

DIRECTORY

the visually and hearing impaired; for a complete list click onto www .metrolisboa.pt. An alternative is the **Carris** (☎ 213 613 141; www.carris.pt) dial-a-ride bus service, which operates on a door-to-door basis from 6.30am to 10pm Monday to Friday and from 8am to 1pm at weekends.

Bookings are required 48 hours in advance and you'll need to show a medical certificate. The airport is fully wheelchair-accessible.

    Accessible Portugal (☎ 919 195 680; www.accessibleportugal.com) can organise city sightseeing, themed tours and equipment rental.

>INDEX

See also separate subindexes for See (p166), Shop (p166), Eat (p167), Drink (p168) and Play (p168).

000 map pages

INDEX

000 map pages